PIZZA

ITALIAN COOKING SCHOOL

PIZZA

THE SILVER SPOON KITCHEN

A TASTE OF ITALY

From humble beginnings when it was founded around 600 BC by a Greek settlement to the ubiquitous presence it has on today's culinary landscape, pizza is arguably Italy's most renowned culinary export. Why? It lends itself to honest and simple flavors; it's an inexpensive food that can be consumed quickly; and it appeals to people of all ages.

With *Italian Cooking School Pizza,* readers learn the fundamentals of preparing pizza and bread doughs to make delicious pizzas, calzones, focaccias, and savory pies. Each chapter starts with a basic recipe, from which you then build up your skills; for example, in the pizza chapter, you start with a pizza dough and develop your technique and palate as you progress through the recipes within the chapter. Eventually, you can prepare delicious meals with confidence.

From a classic Pizza Margherita (see page 21) and a Stuffed Calzone (see page 57) to a Rosemary Focaccia (see page 68) and a Vegetable and Prosciutto Tart (see page 150), the recipes in this book are a celebration of Italian flavors in its truest form. If you're looking to manage your dietary intake and make healthy lifestyle choices, consider substituting ingredients for low-fat or low-sodium options. Enjoy this culinary adventure and invite a little taste of Italy to your home—*buon appetito!*

PIZZA

The basic pizza ingredients are flour, water, salt, and yeast dissolved in lukewarm water. These ingredients are worked into a ball of dough, which should be rested and left to rise (prove) in a warm place for about 3 hours. The dough can be topped according to the pizza recipe—from a White Pizza (see page 22) to a Sausage Pizza (see page 37)—or rolled out and sprinkled with a mixture of oil, water, and salt (half oil to half water) to make a focaccia.

CALZONES

A calzone is a bread that is shaped like folded pizza (and resembles a half moon) and filled with a savory filling. In Italy, calzones are convenient meals or snacks that can be consumed while standing or walking and are often served at delis or by street vendors.

FOCACCIA

We know that the ancient Egyptians, Greeks, and Romans were in the habit of cooking focaccia over a fire (hence the name "focaccia," from the Latin *focus*, meaning "fire"). Like pizza, focaccia is a bread base topped with herbs and other fresh ingredients, but the similarities end there. Traditionally, focaccia contains more leavener in the dough so it has a thicker base, its shape varies, it can be used as an accompaniment for a meal or as pizza or sandwich bread.

SAVORY PIES

The first savory pies date back to 1000 BC. These earliest stuffed pastries were filled with seasoned meat and were cooked directly on the fire. Subsequently, they became larger when a primitive saucepan was lined with bread dough, stuffed with meat, and covered with a lid.

The basic pie dough (shortcrust pastry) is the simplest base for savory pies. All that is needed to make it are flour, butter, and eggs. Mix it quickly with your fingers until you have a smooth dough, wrap it in plastic wrap (clingfilm), and let it rest for 30 minutes to 1 hour in the refrigerator.

The pastry shell (case) for savory pies can be cooked for about 20 minutes at 350°F/180°C/Gas Mark 4 before baking with the filling. To avoid it puffing up as it cooks, prick it with the prongs of a fork or cover it with parchment (baking) paper and fill with pie weights (baking beans), which is then removed after the prebaking. To prevent the pastry from drying out or cracking in the oven, you can put a baking pan of water on the shelf below the pastry.

STRUDELS

Sweet and savory strudels are commonly found in the northern parts of Italy, such as Trentino-Alto Adige, which is bordered by Austria. Strudel is often served as part of a winter tradition.

INGREDIENTS

FLOUR

The right flour will impact the flavor and texture and the best tasting pizzas begin with a good-quality dough. Gluten, a form of protein, creates an elastic texture when wet and creates the chewiness and spring in bread as well as pizza crust (base). While the book encourages the use of traditional Italian flours, such as "o" or "oo," all-purpose (plain) flour is a safe bet (and alternative) for most pizza dough, from deep-dish to thin crust. Strong bread flour is also an ideal option for home pizzas since it tears less than doughs made with all-purpose flour, but it may be more difficult to stretch into shape because of its high gluten content. Classic Neapolitan pizza (see page 19) is made with "oo" flour, a fine Italian flour that lends itself to a thin crust that puffs up around the rim.

WATER

The minerals in water (primarily magnesium and calcium) help to create a bond with a stronger gluten structure, which contributes to the dough's elasticity and chewiness. Although hard water (water with more mineral content) has shown to create a more crispy crust, tap water is perfectly suitable for pizza doughs.

YEAST

Why does pizza or bread dough rise? Because during the resting time, the yeast releases carbon dioxide, just like in sparkling mineral water or sodas. Yeasts are microscopic fungi belonging to the family of saccharomycetes and these "good" microorganisms turn the sugars in flour to alcohol, which then evaporates, and carbon dioxide, which swells the dough.

SALT

The role of salt is to add flavor to the crust and to create a dough that is stronger and less sticky (opposed to dough with low levels of salt, which is more prone to tearing or sticking). Salt also helps to slow down yeast activity during the fermentation process of the dough.

UTENSILS

PARCHMENT (BAKING) PAPER

Parchment (baking) paper enables you to cut down on fat, because it avoids greasing and dusting the baking sheet or pan. This cellulose-base paper is treated with a non-stick coating to withstand high temperatures. It can withstand temperatures up to 430°F/220°C and beyond (this is indicated on the packaging). It can even be used again. To make it stick better to the baking sheet, it can be moistened, squeezed dry, and pressed in place by hand. Any excess can be trimmed with scissors.

BAKING SHEETS OR PANS

Baking sheets or pans are shallow and made of aluminum, flexible silicone, or other nonstick material. They can be round, rectangular, or square, depending on what you plan to cook (or depending on your imagination). The springform kind is convenient, because you can release the sides to make unmolding the pie easier. The classic shape is round, with a diameter of 8–9½ inches/20–24 cm. Ceramic baking pans are also useful because they double up as a serving dishes. Silicone pans withstand temperatures from -72°F/-40°C to 450°F/230°C, making them suitable to go from the freezer directly to the oven.

MOLDS

Made of aluminum or non-stick material, molds are small in size and are suitable for mini-quiches. They can be round (4–6 inches/10–15 cm in diameter) or oval, with smooth or fluted sides. To cut the dough to the correct size for the molds, all you have to do is press down with the mold on the pastry dough and cut out around it, allowing for a bit of overlap.

SPATULAS

Most spatulas are made of silicone and used to gather up, spread, and smooth the surface of the filling on the dough.

PASTRY WHEELS

Pastry wheels are made of stainless steel and enable you to cut pizzas and savory pies easily. You can buy special scissors and spatula sets for cutting and lifting pizza slices.

LONG-HANDLE KNIVES

Whether traditional or ceramic, long-handle knives must never be used directly on the baking sheet or pan.

STEP 1

STEP 2

STEP 3

STEP 4

TECHNIQUE

PASTA DA PANE

BASIC BREAD DOUGH

EASY

– Preparation time: *20 minutes*
  + 2½ hours resting
– Cooking time: *30 minutes*
– Calories per serving: *312*
– *Serves 6*
– *Makes* 1 lb 2 oz/500 g

INGREDIENTS

– ⅜ oz/10 g fresh yeast or
  ½ teaspoons active dry
  yeast
– 4¼ cups (1 lb 2 oz/500 g)
  "0" or strong bread flour
– 1 teaspoon sugar
– 2 tablespoons extra-virgin
– olive oil
– salt

STEP 1

This versatile dough works for many of the recipes in the book. Crumble the yeast into a bowl, add ⅓ cup (1½ oz/40 g) flour, the sugar, and 4 tablespoons water. Stir to mix the ingredients, cover the bowl with a clean cloth, and let the yeast froth to a foam for 20 minutes.

STEP 2

Sift the remaining flour onto a clean work surface, make a well in the center, add the prepared yeast and oil, and sprinkle a teaspoon of salt around the sides. Add ¾ cup (6 fl oz/175 ml) lukewarm water to make a dough. Bring together with your hands and knead for at least 10 minutes, keeping your fingers together as if they were a spatula, and using your thumb to press down on the dough and stretch it. Bang the dough against the work surface occasionally to activate the gluten.

STEP 3

Shape it into a ball, put it in a large, lightly oiled bowl, cut a cross in it, and cover with a clean dish towel. Let rise (prove) in a warm place for at least 2 hours.

STEP 4

Use the dough according to the recipe instructions or to make bread, preheat the oven to 400°F/200°C/Gas Mark 6 and lightly grease two 1-quart/1-liter loaf pans. Punch down the dough without kneading it and divide it in half. Transfer both loaves to the prepared pans. Cover and let rise for another 45 minutes. Score each loaf with a sharp knife and bake for about 30 minutes. Let the loaves rest for 10 minutes and cool completely before cutting.

PIZZA

TECHNIQUE

PIZZA NAPOLETANA
NEAPOLITAN PIZZA

AVERAGE

– Preparation time: *30 minutes*
  + 3 hours resting
– Cooking time: *20 minutes*
– Calories per serving: *704*
– *Serves 4*

FOR THE PIZZA DOUGH

– 1 teaspoon active dry yeast
– scant 1 teaspoon sugar
– 2½ cups (12 oz/350 g)
  "0" flour
– 1¼ cups (5 oz/150 g)
  "00" flour
– 1¼ teaspoons salt

FOR THE TOPPING

– 7 oz/200 g cow's milk
  mozzarella cheese, drained
– 6–7 tablespoons tomato
  passata (strained tomatoes)
– extra-virgin olive oil,
  for drizzling
– a few fresh basil leaves,
  to serve

STEP 1
Dissolve the yeast in a bowl with ⅔ cup (5 fl oz/150 ml) lukewarm water and add the sugar. Sift the flours into a mound in a large bowl or on a clean work surface and make a well in the center. Make a groove around the edge and sprinkle the salt in it. Pour the yeast mixture, 2 tablespoons oil, and another ⅔ cup (5 fl oz/150 ml) lukewarm water into the well.

STEP 2
Mix to make a soft dough and knead until smooth. Shape into a ball, then place in a lightly oiled bowl, cover with plastic wrap (clingfilm), and let rise (prove) in a warm place for about 2 hours. Lightly punch down the dough.

STEP 3
Cover with a slightly damp dishtowel and let rise for 1 hour. Shape the dough ball into a disk with slightly raised edges around a thin central expanse on a large piece of parchment (baking) paper. The dough is ready for use in your recipe.

STEP 4
Preheat the oven to 425°F/220°C/Gas Mark 7. Cut the mozzarella cheese into piece. Spread the tomatoes (tomato passata) on top of the disk, and add a drizzle of oil and the mozzarella. Bake the pizzas for 15–20 minutes. Add a few basil leaves, torn into small pieces, and serve.

PIZZA MARGHERITA

EASY

- Preparation time: *20 minutes*
- Cooking time: *20 minutes*
- Calories per serving: *540*
- *Serves 4*

INGREDIENTS

- 1 quantity Basic Bread Dough (see page 15)
- 2¼ lb/1 kg ripe tomatoes
- 9–11 oz/250–300 g mozzarella cheese
- olive oil, for drizzling
- a few fresh basil leaves
- salt

Preheat the oven to 425°F/220°C/Gas Mark 7 and grease 1 large or 2 small baking sheets.

Bring a pot of water to a boil over high heat, then add the tomatoes and leave them in for 10 seconds. Transfer the tomatoes to a bowl of ice cold water, then skin, seed, and cut them into small pieces and place them in a strainer (sieve) to drain. Slice the mozzarella cheese thinly and set aside.

Roll out the risen dough thinly on a lightly floured surface and spread it out on the baking sheets. Sprinkle the surface with the tomato pieces, remembering to leave a 1-inch/2.5-cm border of dough uncovered around the edge, sprinkle with a little salt and drizzle with a little olive oil. Bake for 15–20 minutes.

Remove the pizza from the oven, arrange a layer of mozzarella slices and small basil leaves on top, return it to the oven, and bake for another 10 minutes, until the uncovered border is golden brown.

Tip: When fresh tomatoes are not in season, use 4 tablespoons tomato puree (passata) instead. If the puree is too runny, reduce it in a skillet or frying pan over high heat until it has thickened. Let cool before using.

PIZZA BIANCA

WHITE PIZZA

– Preparation time: *15 minutes*
– Cooking time: *20 minutes*
– Calories per serving: *529*
– *Serves 4*

INGREDIENTS

– ¾ quantity Basic Bread
  Dough (see page 15)
– 5 oz/150 g mozzarella cheese,
  thinly sliced
– 5 oz/150 g Taleggio cheese,
  thinly sliced
– a few fresh oregano leaves,
  chopped, or 1 generous
  pinch dried oregano
– olive oil, for drizzling
– salt and pepper

Preheat the oven to 425°F/220°C/Gas Mark 7 and line a baking sheet with parchment (baking) paper.

Roll out the dough thinly on a lightly floured surface to fit the baking sheet and top with the slices of mozzarella and Taleggio. Sprinkle with the oregano and season with salt and pepper. Drizzle with olive oil. Bake for about 20 minutes, then remove from the oven and serve.

Tip: If you like a thin crust (base) for your pizza, follow this method. If you prefer a thicker, softer crust, cover the dough and let rise for about 45 minutes after placing it on the baking sheet.

PIZZA ROSSA

TOMATO PIZZA

EASY

– Preparation time: *30 minutes*
– Cooking time: *20–30 minutes*
– Calories per serving: *804*
– *Serves 4*

INGREDIENTS

– 1 quantity Basic Bread
  Dough (see page 15)
– 2¼ lb/1 kg very ripe plum
  tomatoes, chopped
– 4–5 tablespoons olive oil,
  plus extra for greasing
– 2–3 tablespoons fresh basil
  leaves, torn into small pieces
– 2 cloves garlic, finely
  chopped
– 2 tablespoons fresh oregano
  leaves or 1 generous pinch
  dried oregano
– salt

In a large bowl, combine the tomatoes, olive oil, salt, basil leaves, garlic, and oregano. Let stand for at least 30 minutes.

Preheat the oven to 450°F/230°C/Gas Mark 7½ and grease a 10 x 18-inch/25 x 45-cm baking pan.

Drain off the juice released by the tomatoes and dampen the palms of your hands with a little of it. Using the palms of your hands, spread out the dough in the baking pan. Sprinkle the tomato pieces over the surface of the dough, followed by a drizzle of oil. Bake on the lowest shelf of the oven for 30 minutes, or until golden brown.

PIZZELLE FRITTE

FRIED MINI PIZZAS

FOR THE DOUGH

– 1¾ tablespoons active dry
  yeast
– 1 teaspoon sugar or honey
– 4 cups (1 lb 2 oz/500 g)
  "o" flour
– 1 tablespoon olive oil
– 1 teaspoon salt

FOR THE TOPPING

– olive oil, for cooking
– 2 cups (18 fl oz/500 ml)
  tomato puree (passata),
– grated Parmesan cheese

Make the dough. Dissolve the yeast in a bowl with the sugar or honey and a very little lukewarm water, and let stand for a few minutes until frothy. Sift the flour onto a clean work surface, make a well in the center, add the yeast mixture and oil, and sprinkle the salt around the sides. Bring together with your hands and knead, adding enough lukewarm water to make a smooth, elastic dough. Let rise (prove) in an oiled bowl covered with plastic wrap (clingfilm) for 30 minutes, or until it has doubled in volume.

As soon as it is ready, divide the dough into small balls and shape these by hand into small, thin disks for the mini pizzas. Heat plenty of oil in a heavy saucepan and fry the pizzas, in batches, on both sides until golden brown.

Remove with a slotted spatula and drain thoroughly on paper towels. Arrange the mini pizzas in layers in a serving dish and spoon a few tablespoons of tomato puree (passata) and grated cheese over them. Serve immediately.

SFINCIONE

SICILIAN PIZZA

AVERAGE

- Preparation time: *1 hour
  + 1 hour rising*
- Cooking time: *35–40 minutes*
- Calories per serving: *404*
- *Serves 6*

FOR THE DOUGH

- 3 cups (13 oz/ 375 g)
  all-purpose (plain) flour
- 1 teaspoon salt
- 2¼ teaspoons active dry
  yeast
- 1 egg, lightly beaten
- olive oil, for greasing

FOR THE TOPPING

- 2 tablespoons olive oil, plus
  extra for drizzling
- 1 onion, thinly sliced
- 5–6 tomatoes, peeled and
  chopped
- 8 anchovy fillets
- 2 oz/50 g pecorino cheese,
  sliced
- 5 oz/150 g mozzarella
  cheese, sliced
- ⅓ cup (1 oz /25 g) grated
  Parmesan cheese
- ½ cup (2 oz/50 g) pitted
  black olives, chopped
- 3 tablespoons capers,
  rinsed and chopped
- 2 tablespoons coarse
  bread crumbs
- pinch of dried oregano
- pinch of dried red pepper
  (chili) flakes

Sift together the flour, salt and yeast into a large bowl and make a well in the center. Pour 1 cup (8 fl oz/ 250 ml) lukewarm water into the well and stir with a wooden spoon, gradually incorporating the dry ingredients. Add the egg and stir to a soft dough. If the dough is too sticky, add a little more flour. Turn out onto a lightly floured surface and knead for 10 minutes, or until smooth and elastic.

Shape the dough into a ball, place in a lightly oiled bowl and cover with lightly oiled plastic wrap (clingfilm). Let rise (prove) in a warm place for about 1 hour, until almost doubled in size.

Preheat the oven to 220°C/425°F/Gas Mark 7. Brush a baking sheet with oil or line with parchment (baking) paper.

Make the topping. Heat the olive oil in a skillet or frying pan, add the onion, and cook over low heat, stirring occasionally, for 5 minutes, then remove from the heat.

Roll out the dough on a lightly floured surface, then transfer to the baking sheet (alternatively, divide the dough into 6 individual portions). Spread out the tomatoes evenly on top and drizzle with oil. Bake for about 18 minutes. Remove the baking sheet from the oven and sprinkle the onion, anchovies, pecorino, mozzarella, Parmesan, olives, capers, bread crumbs, oregano, and red pepper (chili) flakes over the tomatoes. Drizzle with oil, if necessary, and bake for another 10–15 minutes, until crisp and golden.

PIZZA DI PATATE

POTATO PIZZA

EASY

– Preparation time: *15 minutes*
– Cooking time: *45 minutes*
– Calories per serving: *776*
– *Serves 4*

INGREDIENTS

– ¾ quantity Basic Bread
  Dough (see page 15)
– olive oil, for brushing and
  drizzling
– 3 large waxy potatoes
– 7 oz/200 g pancetta, diced
– scant 1 cup (3½ oz/100 g)
  diced Taleggio cheese
– 2 oz/50 g Parmesan cheese
  shavings
– 1 tablespoon rosemary leaves
– salt and pepper

Preheat the oven to 425°F/220°C/Gas Mark 7 and brush a baking pan with oil. Bring a saucepan of salted water to a boil, add the potatoes, and cook for 12 minutes, or until tender. Drain and let cool, then peel them and cut, them into thin slices.

Spread the dough out in the baking sheet so that it comes a little way up the sides. Fill the dough with the potato slices and drizzle with a little oil.

Bake for about 15 minutes, then add the pancetta and the cheeses, sprinkle with a tablespoon of rosemary leaves, and season with salt and pepper. Return to the oven for 7–8 minutes, then serve hot.

PIZZA AI QUATTRO FORMAGGI

FOUR-CHEESE PIZZA

– Preparation time: *20 minutes*
– Cooking time: *25 minutes*
– Calories per serving: *687*
– *Serves 4*

INGREDIENTS

– ¾ quantity Basic Bread
  Dough (see page 15)
– olive oil, for greasing and
  drizzling
– 2 cups (14 oz/400 g) canned
  Italian tomatoes (such as San
  Marzano), drained, seeded,
  and coarsely chopped
– 3½ oz/100 g mozzarella
  cheese, thinly sliced
– 2½ oz/75 g Gorgonzola
  cheese, thinly sliced
– 2½ oz/75 g fontina cheese,
  thinly sliced
– ⅔ cup (2 oz/50 g) grated
  Parmesan cheese
– salt and pepper

Preheat the oven to 425°F/220°C/Gas Mark 7 and lightly oil a baking sheet, or line it with parchment (baking) paper. Spread out the risen dough thinly on the baking sheet. Sprinkle the pieces of tomato over the surface and sprinkle with a little olive oil.

Bake for about 18 minutes, then cover with the 4 cheeses, sprinkle with a little salt and pepper, and add a drizzle of oil, if necessary. Bake for another 7–8 minutes, until the cheese has melted. Serve hot.

PIZZA GENOVESE

GENOA-STYLE PIZZA

EASY

- Preparation time: *15 minutes*
  + 30 minutes rising
- Cooking time: *40 minutes*
- Calories per serving: *594*
- *Serves 4*

INGREDIENTS

- ¾ quantity Basic Bread
  Dough (see page 15)
- ½ cup (2 oz/50 g) fine
  durum semolina
- ¼ cup (2 fl oz/50 ml)
  olive oil

FOR THE TOPPING

- 2 tablespoons olive oil
- 3 white onions, thinly sliced
- 4 tomatoes, skinned and
  chopped
- 3½ oz/100 g anchovy fillets
- 1 cup (3½ oz/100 g) pitted
  black olives
- 4 cloves garlic
- salt

Work the semolina and oil into the risen dough with
your hands. Knead thoroughly and let rise (prove)
for about 30 minutes.

Preheat the oven to 400°F/200°C/Gas Mark 6 and
brush a baking sheet with oil. Roll out the dough
on a lightly floured surface into a disk about ¾ inch/
2 cm thick and place on the baking pan.

Heat the oil in a saucepan, add the onions, and cook
gently over very low heat until transparent. Add the
tomatoes and season with salt, stir well, and turn
off the heat.

Spread this mixture over the dough and arrange
the anchovy fillets, olives, and the garlic cloves on top.
Bake for about 20 minutes, or until the crust (base)
has browned. Remove and discard the garlic cloves,
then serve.

*Tip: To skin the tomatoes easily, prick their skins in one
or two places, blanch them in boiling water for a few seconds,
drain, plunge them into iced water, then drain again
and remove their skins.*

PIZZA ALLA SALSICCIA

SAUSAGE PIZZA

EASY

– Preparation time: *30 minutes*
– Cooking time: *22 minutes*
– Calories per serving: *420–315*
– *Serves 4*

INGREDIENTS

– olive oil, for brushing
  and drizzling
– 1 quantity Pizza Dough
  (see page 19)
– all-purpose (plain) flour,
  for dusting
– 200 g/7 oz Italian sausages,
  skinned and crumbled
– ⅔ cup (50 g/2 oz) pecorino
  cheese, freshly grated
– 4 tomatoes, peeled and
  chopped
– 3½ oz/100 g smoked
  pancetta, sliced
– 1 teaspoon chopped fresh
  rosemary
– 6 fresh basil leaves, torn
– salt and pepper

Preheat the oven to 220°C/425°F/Gas Mark 7. Brush a baking sheet with olive oil or line with parchment (baking) paper.

Roll out the dough on a lightly floured surface, then press it out on the baking sheet. Sprinkle the tomatoes on top and drizzle with oil. Bake for 20 minutes.

Mix together the sausages and pecorino in a bowl and season with salt and pepper. Sprinkle the sausage mixture on the pizza and top with the pancetta. Sprinkle with the rosemary and basil, drizzle with oil, and bake for another 7–8 minutes.

PIZZA AL PROSCIUTTO CRUDO CON MOZZARELLA

PROSCIUTTO AND MOZZARELLA PIZZA

EASY

– Preparation time: *15 minutes*
– Cooking time: *15–20 minutes*
– Calories per serving: *649*
– *Serves 4*

INGREDIENTS

– 1 lb 2 oz/500 g Basic Bread
  Dough (see page 15)
– olive oil, for greasing and
  drizzling
– 8 thin slices mozzarella
  cheese
– 8 thin slices prosciutto
– salt and pepper

Preheat the oven to 425°F/220°C/Gas Mark 7 and grease a rectangular baking sheet. Wrap each slice of mozzarella cheese in a slice of prosciutto and refrigerate.

Roll out the dough on a lightly floured surface into a rectangle about ⅛ inch/3 mm thick, place on the baking sheet, and sprinkle with a little salt and pepper. Arrange the prosciutto and cheese packages on top in 2 rows of 4 and drizzle oil generously over them.

Bake for 15–20 minutes, then remove and use a sharp knife to cut the pizza vertically in half, then cut each half into 4 pieces, cutting horizontally between the cheese and prosciutto packages. Serve very hot.

Tip: For the prosciutto and cheese packages, try to use a mild prosciutto, such as Parma ham, which will remain tender and subtly flavored.

PIZZA QUATTRO STAGIONI

FOUR SEASONS PIZZA

– Preparation time: *20 minutes*
– Cooking time: *15–20 minutes*
– Calories per serving: *637*
– *Serves 4*

INGREDIENTS

– olive oil, for brushing and drizzling
– 3½ oz/65 g mussels, scrubbed and beards removed
– 1 quantity Pizza Dough (see page 19)
– all-purpose (plain) flour, for dusting
– 4 tomatoes, peeled, seeded, and chopped
– 4 anchovy fillets, halved lengthwise
– ½ cup (2 oz/50 g) green olives
– ⅓ cup (2 oz/50 g) diced, cooked cured ham
– 2 oz/50 g mozzarella cheese, diced
– 4 baby artichokes in oil, drained and halved
– ½ cup (2 oz/50 g) black olives
– salt and pepper

Preheat the oven to 425°F/220°C/Gas Mark 7. Brush a baking sheet with oil or line with parchment (baking) paper.

Discard any mussels with broken shells or that do not shut immediately when sharply tapped. Place in a dry skillet and set over high heat for 2–3 minutes, until they open. Discard any that remain closed. Remove the mussels from their shells.

Roll out the dough on a lightly floured surface, then press it out on the baking sheet. Sprinkle the tomatoes on top and mark out a cross, using the back of a knife. Arrange the anchovy fillets and green olives in one quarter, the mussels in another, the ham and mozzarella in the third, and the artichokes and black olives in the last one. Season with salt and pepper, drizzle with oil, and bake for 15–20 minutes.

PIZZA DI BACCALÀ

SALT COD PIZZA PIE

ADVANCED

– Preparation time: *1 hour +
48 hours soaking + 2¼
hours rising*
– Cooking time: *1 hour*
– Calories per serving: *1080–720*
– *Serves 6–8*

FOR THE DOUGH

– 2 teaspoons active dry
yeast
– 1 tablespoon sugar
– 3⅓ cups (14 oz/400 g) "00"
flour, plus extra for dusting
– ½ cup (4 oz/125 g) lard
– 1¼ teaspoon salt
– pepper

FOR THE FILLING

– 1 lb 2 oz/500 g salted dried
cod, soaked in water for 48
hours and water refreshed
several times
– 3–4 tablespoons olive oil,
plus extra for greasing
– 1 clove garlic
– 8 oz/40 g escarole, shredded
– 2 tablespoons capers
– ¾ cup (2½ oz/70 g) pitted
black olives
– 2 oz/50 g anchovy
fillets
– 1–2 tablespoons finely
chopped fresh flat-leaf parsley

Put the yeast into a bowl with a teaspoon of sugar, mix with ⅔ cup (5 fl oz/150 ml) lukewarm water and let ferment for 10–15 minutes, until frothy. Dissolve the salt in a little lukewarm water.

Using a stand mixer with a dough hook, put the flour into the bowl, add the yeast, lard, remaining sugar, and salt mixture and mix, gradually adding more water as needed to make a smooth dough. Finish kneading by hand on a work surface, adding extra flour if it's too sticky. Shape into a ball, cover, and let rise (prove) at warm room temperature for 2 hours.

Bring a pot of water to a boil over high heat, add the salt cod, then reduce the heat and simmer for 10 minutes. Break into bite-size pieces.

Heat the oil over medium heat in a skillet or frying pan, add the garlic, and cook gently until browned, then remove. Add the escarole and ½ cup (4 fl oz/120 ml) water with half each of the capers and olives, and cook until wilted and most of the water has evaporated.

Preheat the oven to 375°F/190°C/Gas Mark 5 and grease and dust a 9-inch/23-cm round baking pan. Heat a little more oil in a frying pan, add the cod, and cook gently with the remaining capers, olives, and anchovies, and chopped parsley. Stir and let cool.

Punch down the dough and use two-thirds of it to line the bottom and sides of the pan. Place the filling inside and roll out the remaining dough to use as cover over the filling. Fold the dough on the sides of the pan over the top dough and crimp to seal. Brush with olive oil. Let stand for 15 minutes, then bake in the oven for 45 minutes.

PIZZA AI FRUTTI DI MARE

FISHERMAN'S PIZZA

EASY

– Preparation time: *30 minutes*
– Cooking time: *35–40 minutes*
– Calories per serving: *604*
– *Serves 4*

INGREDIENTS

– 11 oz/300 g baby octopuses, cleaned and skinned
– 2 tablespoons olive oil, plus extra for brushing and drizzling
– 11 oz/300 g uncooked shrimp (prawns), peeled and deveined
– 11 oz/300 g clams, scrubbed
– 11 oz/300 g mussels, scrubbed and beards removed
– 1 onion, thinly sliced
– 4 cloves garlic, thinly sliced
– 1 fresh chili, seeded and chopped
– 1 tablespoon chopped flat-leaf parsley
– 1 quantity Pizza Dough (see page 19)
– all-purpose (plain) flour, for dusting
– 2 cups (11 oz/300 g) cherry tomatoes, peeled and quartered
– salt

In a saucepan of salted boiling water, cook the octopuses for 2 minutes, or until tender, then drain well. Preheat the oven to 425°F/ 220°C/Gas Mark 7.

Brush a baking sheet with oil and line it with parchment (baking) paper. Cook the shrimp (prawns) in a saucepan of boiling water for 2–3 minutes, then drain, peel, and devein them. Discard any clams or mussels with broken shells or that do not shut immediately when sharply tapped. Place the remaining clams and mussels in a dry skillet or frying pan and set over high heat for 2–3 minutes, until the shells have opened. Remove the clams and mussels from their shells, discarding any that remain closed.

Heat the oil in a skillet, add the onion, garlic, and chili and cook over low heat, stirring occasionally, for 5 minutes, then add the octopuses, mussels, clams, and shrimp. Season with salt and cook, stirring frequently, for 5 minutes. Remove from the heat and add the parsley.

Roll out the dough on a lightly floured surface, then press it out on the baking sheet. Sprinkle the tomatoes on top, drizzle with oil, and bake for about 15 minutes. Arrange the seafood on top and return the pizza to the oven for another 7–8 minutes (do not overcook the seafood; otherwise, they will become tough).

PIZZA AI PORCINI E FIORI
DI ZUCCA FARCITI

PORCINI AND STUFFED ZUCCHINI FLOWER PIZZA

AVERAGE

– Preparation time: *40 minutes
 + 1 hour chilling*
– Cooking time: *40–45 minutes*
– Calories per serving: *361*
– *Serves 6*

INGREDIENTS

– 1 quantity Pizza Dough
 (see page 19)
– flour, for dusting
– 5 tablespoons olive oil, plus
 extra for drizzling
– 1 small onion, finely chopped
– 6 zucchini (courgettes),
 finely chopped
– 6 zucchini (courgette) flowers
– 3½ oz/100 g fresh porcini
 (cep mushrooms), diced
– 4 oz/120 g mozzarella cheese,
 diced
– 4 sun-dried tomatoes
 preserved in oil, chopped
– salt and pepper

Preheat the oven to 400°F/200°C/Gas Mark 6 and line a 12-inch/30-cm shallow round baking pan with parchment (baking) paper. Roll out the dough into a thin disk on a lightly floured surface and place in the baking pan. Bake for about 10 minutes, then remove and set aside.

Heat 2 tablespoons oil in a saucepan, add the onion and 3 of the zucchini (courgettes), and cook gently for 2–3 minutes, or until the vegetables are tender and excess moisture has evaporated. Season with salt and pepper.

Remove the pistils from the zucchini (courgette) flowers and stuff the flowers with the onion and zucchini mixture. Heat 1 tablespoon oil in a skillet or frying pan, add the mushrooms and cook gently for 10 minutes, moistening them with a little water, if necessary.

Heat 2 tablespoons oil in another pan and gently cook the remaining zucchini, for 2–3 minutes over high heat, stirring frequently and seasoning with salt and pepper.

Mix the mushrooms and zucchini and spread on top of the cooked pizza crust (base) in its baking pan, then arrange the stuffed zucchini flowers on top and sprinkle with the mozzarella cheese. Bake for 5 minutes, then remove and garnish with chopped sun-dried tomatoes, and drizzle with a little oil.

PIZZA DI ORTAGGI

VEGETABLE PIZZA PIE

EASY

– Preparation time: *1 hour
+ 1 hour rising*
– Cooking time: *1 hour
25 minutes*
– Calories per serving: *545*
– *Serves 6*

FOR THE DOUGH

– 2 teaspoons active dry
yeast
– 3½ cups (1 lb 2 oz/500 g)
"0" flour
– ½ cup (4 fl oz/120 ml) oil
– 1½ teaspoons salt

FOR THE FILLING

– 3 eggplants (aubergines),
sliced ¼ inch/5 mm thick
– 2 cloves garlic, sliced
– 1 tablespoon chopped
flat-leaf parsley
– 1 onion, thinly sliced
– scant 1 cup (7 fl oz/200 ml)
vegetable broth (stock)
– ½ red bell pepper, seeded
and chopped
– ½ green bell pepper, seeded
and chopped
– ½ yellow bell pepper,
seeded and chopped
– 2 zucchini (courgettes),
diced
– 2 tablespoons grated
Parmesan cheese
– ⅔ cup (2 oz/60 g) dry
bread crumbs
– 1 egg, lightly beaten

Make the dough. Dissolve the yeast in a bowl with a little of the lukewarm water and let stand for a few minutes until frothy. Sift the flour onto a clean work surface, make a well in the center, add the yeast mixture and oil, and sprinkle the salt around the sides. Bring together with your hands and knead, adding about 1 cup (8 fl oz/250 ml) lukewarm water to make a smooth, elastic dough. Let rise (prove) in an oiled bowl covered with plastic wrap (clingfilm) for 1½ hours, or until it has doubled in volume.

Preheat the oven to 375°F/190°C/Gas Mark 5 and grease a 10-inch/25-cm baking pan. Heat a little oil in a large skillet or frying pan, add the eggplants (aubergines) and one of the garlic cloves, and cook gently until lightly browned and cooked through. Season, sprinkle with parsley, and transfer to a plate. Set aside.

Heat a little more oil in the pan, add the onion and remaining garlic clove, and cook gently over low heat for another 2 minutes. Season with salt and add the broth (stock), then cover and cook for 5 minutes.

Add the bell peppers and cook for 5 minutes, then add the zucchini (courgettes) and eggplants, and cook for another 5 minutes. Remove from the heat and let cool before adding the cheese, bread crumbs, egg, and season with salt.

Roll out two-thirds of the dough on a lightly floured surface and use it to line the baking pan. Layer the vegetables on top and cover with the remaining dough to form a lid. Brush the top with oil and bake for 45 minutes–1 hour. Remove from the oven and serve hot or warm.

PIZZA DI SCAROLA

ESCAROLE PIZZA PIE

AVERAGE

– Preparation time: *30 minutes*
  + 1–2 hours rising
– Cooking time: *1 hour*
– Calories per serving:
  1,140–760
– *Serves 4–6*

FOR THE DOUGH

– 2½ teaspoons active dry
  yeast
– pinch of sugar
– 3 cups (14 oz/400 g)
  strong bread flour
– 1 teaspoon salt
– milk or lukewarm water,
  as necessary
– 1¾ stick (7 oz/200 g) butter

FOR THE FILLING

– 3 lb/900 g escarole, chopped
– 3–4 tablespoons olive oil
– 1 clove garlic
– 3 oz/80 g anchovy fillets,
  rinsed, drained, and
  chopped
– 2 oz/50 g capers, rinsed and
  drained
– ½ cups (5 oz/150 g) black
  olives, pitted and chopped
– 2 tablespoons raisins
  (optional)
– 2 tablespoons pine nuts
– pinch of dried red pepper
  (chili) flakes (optional)
– 1 egg, lightly beaten
– salt and pepper

To make the dough, dissolve the yeast in a small bowl with a pinch of sugar and a little lukewarm water, and let stand for a few minutes until frothy. Sift the flour in a large bowl, make a well in the center, add the yeast mixture, and sprinkle the salt around the sides. Bring together with your hands and knead, adding enough lukewarm water to make a smooth, homogeneous, and not-too-soft dough that can be easily rolled out. Let the dough rise (prove) in an oiled bowl covered with plastic wrap (clingfilm) for 1–2 hours, or until doubled in size.

Meanwhile, bring a saucepan of salted water to a boil, add the escarole, and blanch for about 2 minutes or until just tender, then drain it thoroughly and squeeze it dry. Heat the oil in a skillet or frying pan, add the garlic clove, and cook until golden. Discard the garlic and add the anchovies, capers, olives, raisins, pine nuts, red pepper (chili) flakes, and the escarole. Cook for a few minutes, then remove from the heat, check the seasoning, and let cool.

Roll out the dough on a lightly floured surface into 2 disks. Line a 10-inch/25-cm baking pan with 1 disk of dough, spread the filling over it carefully, then place the other disk on top and crimp the edges to seal. Let it rise for about 1 hour. Preheat the oven to 375°F/190°C/ Gas Mark 5.

Brush the top of the pizza with beaten egg, sprinkle it with salt, and bake for 25–30 minutes. Remove and serve warm or cold.

PIZZA MONTANARA

HAM AND EGG PIZZA PIE

EASY

– Preparation time: *20 minutes*
– Cooking time: *35 minutes*
– Calories per serving: *637*
– *Serves 4*

INGREDIENTS

– 1 quantity Basic Bread
  Dough (see page 15)
– 2 tablespoons olive oil
– 1 large white onion, finely
  chopped
– 9 oz/250 g fontina cheese,
  diced
– 5 oz/150 g Prague ham or
  other quality cooked
  smoked ham, cut into thin
  strips
– 2 eggs, lightly beaten, plus
  1 egg yolk
– salt and pepper

Preheat the oven to 400°F/200°C/Gas Mark 6 and lightly grease a baking sheet. Heat the oil in a saucepan, add the onion, and cook gently until transparent. Add a pinch of salt and remove from the heat.

Divide the dough in half and roll out into 2 disks on a lightly floured surface, one slightly larger than the other. Place the larger disk in the baking pan so that it overlaps the edge and spread out the diced fontina cheese, ham, and the onion over it. Season the two whole eggs with salt and pepper and pour them on top.

Cover with the smaller disk of dough and pinch the edges together to seal. Brush the surface with the egg yolk and bake for 30 minutes, by which time the surface should be golden brown. Remove from the oven and let stand for 5 minutes before serving.

CALZONE

TECHNIQUE

CALZONE FARCITO

STUFFED CALZONE

INGREDIENTS

– 9 oz/250 g mozzarella cheese,
  drained and diced
– ¾ quantity Pizza Dough
  (see page 19)
– ¾ cup (7 oz/200 g)
  tomato puree (passata)
– 1 cup (7 oz/200 g)
  ricotta cheese
– 2 eggs, beaten
– 4 oz/120 g ham, cut into
  strips
– pinch of dried oregano
– pinch of chili powder
– ¼ cup (¾ oz/20 g) grated
  Parmesan cheese
– extra virgin olive oil
– salt and pepper

STEP 1

Divide the risen dough in half and spread each ball out
with your hands to form 2 thin disks, about 10 inches/
25 cm in diameter. Spread out one-third of the tomato
puree (passata) in the center of each one.

STEP 2

Preheat the oven to 425°F/220°C/Gas Mark 7 and line
a baking sheet with parchment (baking) paper. In a
bowl, add the ricotta and gradually stir in the egg. Stir
in the mozzarella, ham, dried oregano, and chili powder.
Season with salt and pepper. Spoon the mixture on the
dough over the tomato puree. Fold each calzone in half,
enclosing the filling to form a half-moon shape, moisten
the edges with a little water, and press them together
to seal.

STEP 3

Brush the tops of the calzone with some of the tomato
puree and bake for 20–25 minutes, until puffed up and
golden brown.

STEP 4

Pour the remaining tomato puree over the calzones,
sprinkle with grated Parmesan cheese, and serve.

*Tip: To seal the calzone, you can press down with a fork
on the edges, or pinch to form a cord-shape edging (see tip
page 59).*

CALZONCELLI

LITTLE PASTIES WITH CHEESE FILLING

EASY

– Preparation time: *15 minutes*
– Cooking time: *25 minutes*
– Calories per serving: *399*
– *Serves 6*

INGREDIENTS

– 1 egg plus 1 egg white,
  lightly beaten
– ¾ cup (7 oz/200 g)
  ricotta cheese
– ¾ cup (2½ oz/60 g) grated
  Parmesan cheese
– 2 oz/50 g ham, coarsely
  chopped
– 5 oz/150 g smoked scamorza
  cheese, diced
– 2 oz/50 g mortadella,
  coarsely chopped
– 1 quantity Basic Bread
  Dough (see page 15)
– flour, for dusting
– salt and pepper
– olive oil, for brushing

Preheat the oven to 400°F/200°C/Gas Mark 6. Put the whole egg, ricotta, Parmesan, and a pinch each of salt and pepper into a food processor and blend. Add the ham, the scamorza, and mortadella and process briefly. Divide the dough into 6 equal balls.

On a lightly floured work surface, roll out the dough balls into 5-inch/13-cm disks. Divide the filling among the disks leaving a 1-inch/2.5-cm border, brush the edges with a little egg white, and fold over the other half, pressing it with a fork around the edges to seal it. Brush lightly with olive oil and bake for about 25 minutes.

Tip: Make a secure and decorative edge once the disks have been folded in half. Simply pinch the edges, making them thinner, then hold the edge between your thumb and index finger and roll it toward the filling for a decorative "corded" border.

CALZONE VEGETARIANO

VEGETARIAN CALZONE

EASY

- Preparation time: *30 minutes*
- Cooking time: *35 minutes*
- Calories per serving: *294*
- *Serves 6*

INGREDIENTS

- 2¼ lb/1 kg escarole or catalogna chicory
- 2 tablespoons olive oil
- 1 clove garlic, crushed
- pinch of dried oregano
- pinch of chili powder
- ⅓ cup (1¼ oz/30 g) grated pecorino cheese, plus extra for brushing
- 1 quantity Basic Bread Dough (see page 15)
- salt

Preheat the oven to 400°F/200°C/Gas Mark 6. Bring a saucepan of salted water to a boil, add the escarole, and cook for 2–3 minutes, then drain it and refresh it quickly under cold running water. Squeeze out the moisture and chop it finely.

Heat the oil in a skillet or frying pan, add the garlic, and lightly brown it before discarding it. Add the escarole, oregano, and chili powder, stir, and cook for 5 minutes. Remove from the heat and stir in the pecorino.

Place the dough on a large disk of parchment (baking) paper and roll or press it out thinly to cover the disk.

Place the escarole mixture on one half of the dough disk and fold over the other half to enclose it, pinching all along the edges with your fingertips to seal them. Prick the surface with a fork, brush with oil, and bake for about 25 minutes. Remove from the oven, let stand for 5 minutes, and serve warm.

Tip: If the dough is too dry to make a good seal around the edges, use a pastry brush dipped in water to dampen the edges, then press them firmly closed.

CALZONI ALLA TURCA

TURKISH-STYLE CALZONE

EASY

- Preparation time: *15 minutes*
- Cooking time: *20 minutes*
- Calories per serving: *406*
- *Serves 6*

INGREDIENTS

- olive oil, for brushing
- sprig of fresh mint
- 1¼ cups (11 oz/300 g)
  ricotta or quark cheese
- 1 small clove garlic, very
  finely chopped
- 1 quantity Basic Bread
  Dough (see page 15)
- flour, for dusting
- salt and pepper

Preheat the oven to 400°F/200°C/Gas Mark 6 and brush a baking sheet with oil. Chop the mint coarsely and stir it into the ricotta or quark in a bowl. Beat well with a wooden spoon, then stir in the garlic clove and season with salt and pepper.

Roll out the dough into a thin layer on a lightly floured surface and cut out twelve 4-inch/10-cm disks. Place a little of the ricotta cheese mixture on one half of each disk, fold over the other half to cover the filling, and press the edges closed with your fingertips. Place the pasties on the baking sheet and bake for 20 minutes, then remove and serve.

Tip: If you use ricotta, you can thin it out by mixing 3–4 tablespoons yogurt. For extra flavor, add chopped basil leaves to the filling.

FOCACCIA

TECHNIQUE

FOCACCIA GENOVESE
GENOA-STYLE FOCACCIA

AVERAGE

– Preparation time: *30 minutes
+ 2½ hours rising*
– Cooking time: *20 minutes*
– Calories per portion: *197*
– *Serves 6*

INGREDIENTS

– 2¾ cups (12 oz/350 g) "00"
flour
– 1 teaspoon salt
– 2¼ teaspoons active dry
yeast
– 1 teaspoon honey
– 4 teaspoons extra virgin olive
oil, plus 3½ tablespoons for
baking

STEP 1

Sift the flour into a mound on a clean work surface
and make a well in the center. Make a groove around
the edge and sprinkle over the salt. Dissolve the yeast
with 2 teaspoons lukewarm water and the honey. Pour
this mixture into the well. Add the 4 teaspoons oil and
another scant ½ cup (3½ fl oz/100 ml) water and stir
with your fingers, gradually incorporating the flour from
the sides of the well to form a soft dough.

STEP 2

Knead for about 10 minutes, then shape it into a ball,
put it in a lightly oiled bowl, cut a cross in the top, cover,
and let rise (prove) in a warm place for about 1 hour.
Transfer to a work surface and lightly punch the dough
down. Pour 2 tablespoons oil onto the middle of a 8 x 12
inch/20 x 30 cm baking pan and place the dough on top.
Fill the entire baking pan with the dough, pressing it out
with your hands. Sprinkle with a generous pinch of sea
salt on top, cover with 2 sheets of aluminum foil in a tent
shape, and let rise in a warm place for 30 minutes.

STEP 3

Preheat the oven to 450°F/230°C/Gas Mark 8. Mix scant
½ cup (3½ fl oz/100 ml) water with 3½ tablespoons oil,
pour it over the dough, and push down on the dough
with your fingertips to make several deep holes right to
the bottom of the pan. Let the focaccia rise in a warm
place for another 1 hour.

STEP 4

Bake for about 20 minutes, or until the top is golden
brown. Let cool, then serve in chunks.

FOCACCIA AL ROSMARINO

ROSEMARY FOCACCIA

EASY

– Preparation time: *35 min*
 + *1 hour rising*
– Cooking time: *50 minutes*
– Calories per serving: *374–281*
– *Serves 6-8*

INGREDIENTS

– 2 tablespoons olive oil,
  plus extra for brushing
– 1 teaspoon superfine (caster)
  sugar
– 1 cup (8 fl oz/250 ml)
  lukewarm milk
– 2½ teaspoons active dry
  yeast
– 3 cups (14 oz/400 g) strong
  white bread or 3¼ cups
  (14 oz/400 g) all-purpose
  (plain) flour, plus extra for
  dusting
– 2 teaspoons salt
– 2 sprigs rosemary,
  coarsely chopped
– coarse sea salt

Brush a large baking sheet with oil or line with baking parchment (baking) paper. Dissolve the sugar in the warm milk in a bowl, sprinkle the yeast over the surface, and let stand for 10–15 minutes, until frothy. Stir well to make a smooth paste.

Sift together the flour and salt into a bowl. Stir in the yeast, rosemary, and oil. Mix well, turn out onto a lightly floured surface, and knead for 10 minutes, or until smooth and elastic.

Roll out to a 9-inch/23-cm disk and carefully place on the prepared baking sheet. Using your fingertip, make 10 dimples in the surface of the dough and insert 2–3 grains of coarse salt in each. Brush with the oil and let rise (prove) in a warm place for 1 hour.

Preheat the oven to 400°F/200°C/Gas Mark 6. Bake the loaf for 30 minutes, until deep golden brown. Remove from the oven, transfer to a wire rack to cool slightly, and serve warm.

FOCACCIA CON OLIVE

OLIVE FOCACCIA

EASY

– Preparation time: *15 minutes*
– Cooking time: *30 minutes*
– Calories per serving: *208*
– *Serves 4*

INGREDIENTS

– 1 quantity Basic Bread
  Dough (see page 15)
– flour, for dusting
– 2 tablespoons olive tapenade
– olive oil, for greasing and
  drizzling
– 1½ cups (5 oz/150 g) green
  and black olives, pitted
– coarse sea salt

Knead the bread dough for 2 minutes on a floured board. Dilute the olive tapenade with a drizzle of oil and work it into the dough. Cover and let rest in a warm place for about 30 minutes, then flatten it gently and roll it out on a lightly floured surface to a thickness of ¼ inch/5 mm. Preheat the oven to 475°F/240°C/Gas Mark 9 and grease a baking pan.

Spread out the dough in the baking pan and prick the surface with a fork, space out the whole olives on it, and sprinkle with a pinch of salt. Drizzle a very little oil over the surface and bake for about 30 minutes. Remove from the oven, rest it for 5 minutes, then serve.

FOCACCIA AGLI AROMI VERDI
HERB FOCACCIA

INGREDIENTS

– 1 quantity Basic Bread
  Dough (see page 15)
– 2 tablespoons olive oil,
  plus extra for brushing
– fresh basil leaves, finely
  chopped
– fresh flat-leaf parsley,
  finely chopped
– coarse sea salt

Preheat the oven to 400°F/200°C/Gas Mark 6 and brush a pizza pan with oil. Work the olive oil into the dough and knead very thoroughly until smooth and elastic. Add the basil and parsley and knead until these are evenly distributed.

Spread out the dough in the pan, using your fingertips, so that it fills the pan to a thickness of ¼ inch/6 mm. Brush the surface with oil, sprinkle sparingly with salt, and bake for about 25 minutes.

Remove from the oven and let stand for 5 minutes, then serve.

FOCACCIA ALLA SCAROLA

ESCAROLE FOCACCIA

EASY

– Preparation time: *20 minutes*
– Cooking time: 30–35 *minutes*
– Calories per serving: *382*
– *Serves 8*

INGREDIENTS

– 1 quantity Basic Bread
  Dough (see page 15)
– 2 tablespoons olive oil
– 14 oz/400 g escarole, cut
  into thin strips
– 4 anchovy fillets, chopped
– 7 oz/200 g caciotta or
  Taleggio cheese, cut into
  ⅛-inch/3-mm slices
– salt and pepper

Preheat the oven to 425°F/220°C/Gas Mark 7 and line a 10-inch/25-cm diameter baking pan with parchment (baking) paper. Divide the dough in half and roll both pieces out into disks on a lightly floured surface, one slightly larger than the baking pan and the other one smaller and thinner. Set aside to rest for a few minutes.

Meanwhile, heat the oil in a saucepan, add the escarole, and cook for 5 minutes, seasoning with salt and pepper.

Place the larger disk of dough in the baking pan, so that the edges come a little way up the sides. Prick the bottom with a fork, spread the escarole over it, distribute the anchovies on top, and follow with a layer of cheese. Cover with the smaller disk of dough and press the edges together to seal. Prick the top layer with a fork and brush with oil.

Bake for 25–30 minutes until golden brown, then remove and let rest for 2 minutes. Transfer to a serving dish and serve.

Tip: Escarole releases a lot of moisture when cooked. If there is still liquid in the pan when the cooking time has elapsed, turn up the heat and continue cooking, stirring, until it has evaporated.

FOCACCIA CON PECORINO
E SALVIA

FOCACCIA WITH SAGE AND PECORINO CHEESE

AVERAGE

– Preparation time: *20 minutes*
– Cooking time: *25 minutes*
– Calories per serving: *342*
– *Serves 6*

INGREDIENTS

– 1 quantity Basic Bread
  Dough (page 15)
– 2 tablespoons olive oil,
  plus extra for greasing and
  sprinkling
– 10 fresh sage leaves, torn into
  very small pieces
– ⅓ cup (1¼ oz/30 g) coarsely
  grated pecorino cheese
– fairly coarse sea salt

Preheat the oven to 400°F/200°C/Gas Mark 6 and grease a rectangular baking pan. Work the oil into the dough and add the sage leaves. Knead thoroughly. Spread the dough out by hand into the pan, pushing it with your fingertips so that it fills the pan to a thickness of ⅛ inch/ 4 mm. Sprinkle very sparingly with oil and sea salt and bake for 15 minutes.

Remove from the oven, sprinkle with the pecorino, and return to the oven for another 10 minutes. Serve.

Tip: If the sage leaves are not very small and tender, use scissors to cut out and discard the tough central rib from each leaf.

FOCACCIA COLORATA

TRICOLOR VEGETABLE FOCACCIA

EASY

- Preparation time: *30 minutes + 30 minutes rising*
- Cooking time: *25 minutes*
- Calories per serving: *349*
- *Serves 8*

FOR THE FOCACCIA

- 1½ tablespoons active dry yeast
- 3 cups (12 oz/350 g) all-purpose (plain) flour
- 1¼ cups (5 oz/150 g) buckwheat flour
- 1 teaspoon salt

FOR THE FILLING

- 7 oz/200 g pumpkin, cubed
- pinch of freshly grated nutmeg
- scant 1 cup (7 oz/200 g) ricotta cheese
- ⅔ cup (2 oz/50 g) grated Parmesan cheese
- 5 cups (9 oz/250 g) spinach, finely chopped
- flour, for dusting
- olive oil, for greasing
- salt and pepper

To make the dough, dissolve the yeast in a bowl with a little lukewarm water and let stand for a few minutes until frothy. Sift both types of flour onto a clean work surface and make a well in the center. Add the yeast mixture and sprinkle the salt around the sides. Bring together with your hands and knead, adding enough lukewarm water to make a smooth, elastic dough. Let rise (prove) in an oiled bowl covered with plastic wrap (clingfilm), for 30 minutes, or until it has doubled in volume.

Preheat the oven to 400°F/200°C/Gas Mark 6 and lightly grease a 9-inch/23-cm baking pan. Bring a saucepan of water to a boil, steam the pumpkin until tender, then process to a puree in a food processor. Add the nutmeg, salt, and pepper.

In a separate bowl, combine the ricotta, Parmesan, and chopped spinach.

Roll the dough out on a lightly floured surface to make 2 disks and place one in the baking pan. Cover it with a layer of pumpkin, followed by a layer of the ricotta mixture, keeping the 2 layers well defined. Place the second disk of dough on top, pinch the edges firmly together to seal and bake for 25 minutes. Remove from the oven, let cool a little, and serve warm.

Tip: If you use quark instead of ricotta, you can mix it with 3–4 tablespoons yogurt if it needs thinning slightly. For extra flavor, try adding a few basil leaves to the cheese filling.

FOCACCIA DI CIPOLLE

ONION FOCACCIA

AVERAGE

– Preparation time: *20 minutes
  + 1 hour rising*
– Cooking time: *40 minutes*
– Calories per serving: *486*
– *Serves 4*

FOR THE FOCACCIA

– 2½ teaspoons active dry
  yeast
– ½–¾ cup (4–6 fl oz/
  120–175 ml) milk
– generous 2 cups (9 oz/250 g)
  "o" flour
– 1 egg
– olive oil, for greasing

FOR THE TOPPING

– 4 tablespoons (2 oz/50 g)
  butter, plus extra for
  greasing
– 2 large red onions, finely
  chopped
– sprig of fresh flat-leaf
  parsley, finely chopped
– salt

Dissolve the yeast in a little lukewarm milk, add just enough flour to form a small soft ball, and let rest for 1 hour. Sift the remaining flour into a mound on a clean work surface, make a well in the center, break the egg into it, add the risen dough ball, and work it into the flour, adding enough milk to yield a soft dough. Shape into a ball, transfer to a lightly greased bowl, cover with plastic wrap (clingfilm), and let rise for 1 hour.

Preheat the oven to 350°F/180°C/Gas Mark 4 and grease a baking pan with butter. Melt the butter in a saucepan, add the onions, and fry gently. Season with salt and add the parsley. Add all but 2–3 tablespoons of this mixture to the risen dough, kneading it briefly and quickly, then spread out in the baking pan.

Spread the remaining onion mixture over the surface, cover with foil, and bake for 20 minutes. Remove the foil and bake for another 10 minutes, until the onions are browned. Remove and serve hot.

FOCACCIA PUGLIESE

PUGLIAN FOCACCIA

EASY

– Preparation time: *20 minutes
+ 1½ hours rising*
– Cooking time: *25 minutes*
– Calories per serving: *428*
– *Serves 6*

INGREDIENTS

– 1 potato
– 2 teaspoons active dry yeast
– 1 teaspoon sugar
– 2 cups (9 oz/250 g) "00"
  flour
– 4–5 tablespoons extra-virgin
  olive oil
– 12 cherry tomatoes
– pinch of dried oregano
– salt

Cut the potato into chunks and steam them for 15 minutes, until tender. Mash it until smooth and let cool.

Crumble the yeast into a bowl with the sugar and dissolve it in ⅔ cup (5 fl oz/150 ml) lukewarm water. Sift the flour into a mound in a large bowl or a clean work surface and make a well in the center, add the potato, pour the dissolved yeast into the middle, and mix together to form a smooth and soft dough. Transfer to a lightly oiled bowl, cover with plastic wrap (clingfilm), and let rise (prove) in a warm place until doubled in volume.

Lightly grease a 13½-inch/34-cm baking sheet. Transfer the dough to the baking sheet, pour over 2–3 tablespoons oil, and press the dough out with your hands until it is the same size as the sheet. Push the cherry tomatoes deep into the dough, sprinkle the oregano on top, and season with salt. Cover the focaccia and let rise for another hour.

Preheat the oven to 400°F/200°C/Gas Mark 6. Whisk 1 tablespoon water with the remaining 2 tablespoons oil and brush it over the dough. Bake for 25 minutes.

Tip: Avoid adding the yeast at the same time as the salt, because the salt interferes with the fermentation of the enzymes in the yeast if in direct contact. Begin by combining the yeast and its liquid together with the flour, and only after this season with salt.

FOCACCINE ALLA PANCETTA

MINI PANCETTA FOCACCIAS

EASY

– Preparation time: *20 minutes*
– Cooking time: *40 minutes*
– Calories per serving: *502*
– *Serves 6*

INGREDIENTS

– ¾ quantity Basic Bread
  Dough (see page 15)
– 1 tablespoon olive oil, plus
  extra for greasing and
  cooking
– 10 fresh mint leaves,
  chopped
– 7 oz/200 g pancetta or
  bacon, chopped
– 5 oz/150 g semi-soft, young
  Sardinian pecorino cheese,
  chopped
– 1 egg yolk, lightly beaten

Preheat the oven to 350°F/180°C/Gas Mark 4 and grease a baking sheet. Work the mint leaves finely into the dough, kneading well. Heat 1 tablespoon oil in a saucepan, add the pancetta, and cook gently until browned. Drain off any oil and let cool. Add the cheese and egg yolk to the saucepan, then incorporate into the dough. Knead well for at least 10 minutes.

Divide the dough into small portions and, dipping your fingers in water, shape them into little focaccias, each one about ¾ inch/2 cm thick. Place on the baking sheet and bake for about 30 minutes.

Tip: If you have a food processor with a dough hook attachment, you can use it to combine all the flavoring ingredients evenly with the dough.

FOCACCIA DI RECCO

RECCO-STYLE FOCACCIA

EASY

– Preparation time: *20 minutes*
– Cooking time: *15 minutes*
– Calories per serving: *333*
– *Serves 6*

INGREDIENTS

– ¾ quantity Basic Bread
  Dough (see page 15)
– 1½ tablespoons olive oil, plus
  extra for greasing brushing
– 11 oz/300 g crescenza or
  Taleggio cheese, thinly sliced

Preheat the oven to 485°F/250°C/Gas Mark 9½ and grease a baking sheet. Work the oil into the dough, kneading until it is smooth and elastic. Divide the dough in half and roll it out into 2 thin equal disks. Place one piece on the baking sheet and cover the surface with the crescenza cheese, leaving a ¾-inch/2-cm border around the edge. Cover with the second disk and pinch the edges tightly to seal to prevent the cheese from oozing out as it cooks.

Prick the surface with the prongs of a fork, brush with oil, and bake for 15 minutes. Remove and serve piping hot.

Tip: You can prevent the focaccia from puffing up excessively as it cooks by tearing fairly large holes here and there in the upper layer of dough with your fingertips, allowing for the steam to escape.

FOCACCINE CON SALSA DI FETA

FOCACCIA WITH FETA

EASY

– Preparation time: *40 minutes*
+ 40 minutes rising
– Cooking time: *10 minutes*
– Calories per serving: *698*
– *Serves 4*

FOR THE FOCACCIA

– 2½ teaspoons active dry
yeast
– 1 teaspoon sugar
– 2 cups (9 oz/250 g)
all-purpose (plain) flour
– 2 cups (9 oz/250 g)
whole wheat (wholemeal)
flour
– 2 tablespoons olive oil, plus
extra for greasing

FOR THE
CHEESE SPREAD

– 1⅔ cups (9 oz/250 g)
crumbled Greek feta cheese
– milk, as required
– 3 tablespoons olive oil
– pinch of chili powder
– ¼ cup (1½ oz/40 g) cream
cheese

Pour 1 cup (8 fl oz/250 ml) lukewarm water into a bowl
and add the yeast and sugar. Set aside to ferment
in a warm place for 5–6 minutes. Sift both flours
together into a mound in a large bowl or on a clean
work surface, make a well in the center, add the yeast
mixture and oil, and bring it together with your hands,
kneading to form a smooth and elastic dough. Shape
into a ball, place in an oiled bowl, cover with plastic
wrap (clingfilm), and rise (prove) in a warm place
for 30 minutes.

Preheat the oven to 485°F/250°C/Gas Mark 9½ and line
several baking sheets with parchment (baking) paper.
Punch down the dough to knock out the air and divide
it into 12 equal portions. Shape these into balls, then roll
them out into disks about ¼ inch/5 mm thick and place
on the baking sheets. Use a pastry brush to dampen
the tops with water and drizzle each with a little oil. Let
rest for 15 minutes, then bake for 7–8 minutes.

Meanwhile, make the cheese spread. Process the feta
cheese with a little milk in a blender, add the oil a little
at a time until smooth and creamy, then add the chili
powder and the cream cheese. Blend for a few more
minutes. Serve the focaccia with the spread
as an appetizer (starter).

FOCACCIA ALLA FORMAGGETTA

CHEESE FOCACCIA

AVERAGE

– Preparation time: *30 minutes
+ 30 minutes rising*
– Cooking time: *15–20 minutes*
– Calories per serving: *355*
– *Serves 6*

INGREDIENTS

– 1 quantity Basic Bread
  Dough (see page 15)
– 1 lb 2 oz/500 g semi-soft
  Ligurian cheese (formagetta
  ligure), thinly sliced
– olive oil, for brushing and
  drizzling
– coarse salt and table salt

Preheat the oven to 400°F/200°C/Gas Mark 6 and brush a baking pan with oil. Knead the dough again for a few minutes, divide into 2 halves, and roll these out on a lightly floured surface into thin layers about the same size as the pan.

Place one of the dough layers in the pan, distribute the cheese slices on top, and cover with the other dough layer, pinching the edges tightly closed and rolling them upward and over toward the center to make a "corded" edging (see tip on page 59). Prick the surface with a fork, cover the pan with a clean dish towel, and let rise again for about 30 minutes.

Brush the surface of the focaccia with oil and sprinkle with coarse sea salt. Bake for 15–20 minutes, or until the surface has browned. Remove from the oven, transfer to a serving dish, and serve hot.

FOCACCIA ALLA PANCETTA E PECORINO
PANCETTA AND PECORINO FOCACCIA

EASY

– Preparation time: *15 minutes*
– Cooking time: *15 minutes*
– Calories per serving: *459*
– *Serves 6*

FOR THE FOCACCIA

– ¾ quantity Basic Bread Dough (see page 15)
– 10 fresh sage leaves, finely chopped
– 1 tablespoon olive oil, plus extra for brushing
– 2 cups (5 oz/150 g) grated pecorino cheese
– 1 egg
– 7 oz/200 g smoked pancetta, diced
– pepper

FOR THE SALAD

– 11 oz/300 g baby spinach leaves
– olive oil, to taste
– wine vinegar, to taste
– salt

Preheat the oven to 425°F/220°C/Gas Mark 7 and line a 10-inch/25-cm baking pan with parchment (baking) paper. Knead the sage leaves into the bread dough and set aside.

Heat the oil in a saucepan, add the pancetta, and cook until lightly browned. Drain off the oil. Mix the pecorino with the egg in a bowl, add the pancetta, and season with pepper.

Divide the dough in half and roll out on a lightly floured surface to form 2 disks, one slightly larger than the other. Place the large disk in the baking pan so that the edges come a little way up the sides. Prick the bottom with a fork and cover with the cheese, egg, and pancetta mixture. Cover with the smaller disk and pinch the edges firmly to seal them. Prick the top with a fork and brush it with oil. Bake for 15 minutes.

Meanwhile, make the spinach salad by dressing the leaves with oil, wine vinegar, and salt. Remove the focaccia and let rest for a few minutes, then transfer to a serving dish and serve with the spinach salad on the side.

FOCACCIA ALLO STRACCHINO

STRACCHINO CHEESE FOCACCIA

AVERAGE

– Preparation time: *15 minutes*
– Cooking time: *20 minutes*
– Calories per serving: *306*
– *Serves 6*

INGREDIENTS

– generous 2 cups (9 oz/250 g)
  "00" flour
– 1 tablespoon olive oil
– 7 oz/200 g stracchino
  cheese, sliced
– table salt
– coarse sea salt

Preheat the oven to 475°F/240°C/Gas Mark 9 and line a baking sheet with parchment (baking) paper. Sift the flour into a mound on a clean work surface, make a well in the center, and pour the oil into it, followed by a pinch of salt, and add a scant ½ cup (3½ fl oz/100 ml) water to make a soft dough (add a little more water if necessary). Bring together with your hands and knead well until soft and elastic, then set aside.

Divide the dough in half and roll both halves into thin disks. Place a disk on the baking sheet, prick it with a fork, and cover with the cheese slices, leaving a ¾-inch/2-cm border around the edge. Sprinkle sparingly with table salt and cover it with the second disk of dough, then pinch firmly all around the edge to seal. Prick the surface with a fork, brush with oil, and press coarse sea salt into the dough, well spaced out. Bake for 15–20 minutes.

FOCACCIA DI ZUCCA

PUMPKIN FOCACCIA

AVERAGE

– Preparation time: *30 minutes
+ 15 minutes rising*
– Cooking time: *1 hour
15 minutes*
– Calories per serving: *277*
– *Serves 6*

INGREDIENTS

– 2 cups (7 oz/200 g) diced
pumpkin
– 3¼ teaspoons active dry
yeast
– 2½ cups (1 oz/300 g) "o"
flour
– 2 tablespoons olive oil, plus
extra for brushing
– 1 red onion, sliced very
thinly into rings
– 1–2 heads red Treviso
radicchio (chicory),
thinly sliced
– salt

Bring a saucepan of water to a boil and steam the
pumpkin for 20–30 minutes. Drain well, place in a bowl,
and mash with a fork to form a puree. Let cool.

Preheat the oven to 350°F/180°C/Gas Mark 4 and brush
an 8-inch/20-cm square baking pan with oil. Dissolve
the yeast in a little lukewarm water and let stand until
frothy. Mix the pumpkin puree with the flour and add
the yeast mixture and a pinch of salt. Knead well
and let rise (prove) for 15 minutes.

Meanwhile, heat the oil in a saucepan, add the onion,
and cook gently until transparent, then remove from
the oil and set aside. Add the red Treviso radicchio
(chicory) to the pan and cook gently until it has wilted.

Spread out the dough in the baking pan to a thickness
of ½ inch/1 cm. Sprinkle the onion rings and the
radicchio on the surface and bake for 45 minutes.

FOCACCIA AL RADICCHIO ROSSO

RADICCHIO FOCACCIA

EASY

– Preparation time: *15 minutes*
  + 30 minutes resting
– Cooking time: *35 minutes*
– Calories per serving: *370*
– *Serves 6*

INGREDIENTS

– 1 quantity Basic Bread
  Dough (see page 15)
– 2 tablespoons olive oil, plus
  extra for brushing
– 14 oz/400 g radicchio, cut
  into thin strips
– ½ cup (2 oz/60 g) grana
  padano cheese shavings
– salt

Knead the bread dough and incorporate the olive oil until it is smooth and elastic. Cover with a clean dish towel and let rise (prove) for 30 minutes.

Preheat the oven to 400°F/200°C/Gas Mark 6 and grease a baking pan.

Heat the olive oil in a saucepan and gently cook the radicchio for 10 minutes. Season with salt and set aside.

Roll out the dough into 2 disks, one slightly larger than the other. Line the pan with the larger disk, spread the radicchio on the surface, and sprinkle with the shavings of cheese. Cover with the smaller disk, pinching the edges together tightly. Prick the lid in several places with a fork and brush it with oil.

Bake for 25 minutes, or until the surface is golden brown. Remove from the oven and let rest for 5 minutes before serving.

Tip: For perfect shavings, use a vegetable peeler and choose a sharp (semimature) grana padano, not a hard, mature one.

PISCIALANDREA

ONION, ANCHOVY, AND BLACK OLIVE FOCACCIA

EASY

– Preparation time: *15 minutes*
  + 30 minutes resting
– Cooking time: *50 minutes*
– Calories per serving: *518*
– *Serves 6*

INGREDIENTS

– 4–5 tablespoons extra-virgin
  olive oil
– 1 clove garlic, crushed
– 2 small sprigs fresh thyme
– 1 bay leaf
– 6–7 yellow onions,
  very thinly sliced
– 1 teaspoon sugar
– 15 anchovy fillets
– 24 olives
– ¾ quantity Basic Bread
  dough (see page 15)
– salt and pepper

Heat the oil in a skillet or frying pan and add the garlic, thyme, bay leaf, onions, and sugar. Season with salt and cook, covered, over low heat, for about 30 minutes, stirring occasionally, until the onions are soft. Discard the garlic, thyme, and bay leaf. Chop 6–7 of the anchovy fillets and stir them in until they have dissolved.

Preheat the oven to 425°F/220°C/Gas Mark 7 and line an 8 x 12-inch/20 x 30-cm baking sheet with parchment (baking) paper. Roll out the dough into a fairly thick rectangle and transfer to the baking sheet. Slice the remaining anchovy fillets into thin strips.

Spread the onion mixture on top of the dough, add the sliced anchovy fillets in a large lattice pattern, and add the olives. Bake for about 25 minutes, then remove and let cool. Serve cold.

Tip: If you are using already prepared bread dough that has still to be rolled out, take it out of the refrigerator 30 minutes before you need it. Do not knead it, but roll it out directly with a rolling pin to avoid reactivating the gluten, which makes it difficult to roll out and more likely to shrink.

SAVORY
PIES

TECHNIQUE

TORTA SALATA
HAM AND CHEESE TART

EASY

– Preparation time: *45 minutes + 1 hour chilling*
– Cooking time: *55 minutes*
– Calories per portion: *492*
– *Serves 6*

FOR THE BASIC PIE DOUGH (SHORTCRUST PASTRY)

– 1⅔ cups (7 oz/200 g) all-purpose (plain) flour
– 7 tablespoons (3½ oz/100 g) butter, chilled and cut into cubes, plus extra for greasing
– salt

FOR THE FILLING

– 4 oz/120 g smoked pancetta or bacon, finely diced
– 2 eggs, plus 2 egg yolks
– ⅔ cup (5 fl oz/150 ml) heavy (double) cream
– ⅔ cup (5 fl oz/150 ml) milk
– ¾ cup (3½ oz/100 g) grated Gruyère cheese
– pinch of freshly grated nutmeg
– salt and pepper

STEP 1
Sift the flour into a mound in a large bowl or on a clean work surface, make a well in the center, and add a pinch of salt and the butter. Rub the butter into the flour with your fingertips, until it resembles bread crumbs. Work quickly to avoid heating the mixture too much.

STEP 2
Mound up the mixture again, make a well in the center, and pour about 3½ tablespoons cold water to make a dough. Handle the dough as little as possible to avoid overheating the mixture. (If handled excessively, it will be tough, dry, and hard.) Bring it together, flatten into a disk, wrap it in plastic wrap (clingfilm), and let chill in the refrigerator for at least 30 minutes.

STEP 3
Roll out the dough on a lightly floured work surface, lift it over the rolling pin, and transfer it to a shallow 9½-inch/24-cm tart pan. Press the sides and the bottom down and trim off any overlap. Put the pan into the refrigerator to chill for about 30 minutes, until firm.

STEP 4
Preheat the oven to 350°F/180°C/Gas Mark 4 and place a lipped baking sheet in the oven to heat. Cook the pancetta or bacon in a nonstick skillet or frying pan for 5–10 minutes, until lightly browned. Remove and drain on paper towels. Beat the eggs and egg yolks with the cream, milk, and cheese, and season with nutmeg, salt, and pepper. Arrange the pancetta or bacon in the shell (case), pour over the egg mixture, and cook at on the lowest shelf of the oven for 45 minutes. Serve warm.

CROSTATA SALATA

SIMPLE TART

EASY

– Preparation time: *10 minutes*
– Cooking time: *30 minutes*
– Calories per serving: *474*
– *Serves 6*

INGREDIENTS

– 1 quantity Basic Pie Dough
  (Shortcrust Pastry), see
  page 105
– all-purpose (plain) flour, for
  dusting
– 3 eggs
– 2 tablespoons heavy
  (double) cream
– 2½ tablespoons grated mild
  pecorino cheese
– 7 oz/200 g mozzarella
  cheese, finely diced
– 5 oz/150 g ham, finely diced
– 3½ oz/100 g mortadella,
  finely diced
– salt

Preheat the oven to 375°F/190°C/Gas Mark 5 and line
a 10-inch/25-cm baking sheet with parchment
(baking) paper.

Roll out the dough to a large disk on a lightly floured
work surface and transfer to the prepared baking sheet,
leaving a ½-inch/1-cm overhang around the edge of the
sheet.

To make the filling, beat the eggs in a bowl, stir in
the cream, pecorino cheese, mozzarella cheese, ham,
and mortadella. Season with salt.

Spread the filling over the dough and fold over the
dough that overlaps the edge to contain it. Press it
down on the filling with the prongs of a fork to make
a border. Bake for 30 minutes, then let stand for a few
minutes before serving.

TORTA SALATA DI POMODORI ALLA SENAPE

TOMATO AND MUSTARD TART

EASY

– Preparation time: *15 minutes*
 + 30 minutes chilling
– Cooking time: *40 minutes*
– Calories per portion: *380*
– *Serves 6*

INGREDIENTS

– 9 ripened tomatoes
– ¾ quantity Basic Pie Dough
 (Shortcrust Pastry), see
 page 105
– 2 tablespoons Dijon mustard
– ¾ cup (3½ oz/100 g)
 coarsely grated Gruyère
 cheese
– 1 teaspoon dried herbes de
 Provence
– extra-virgin olive oil, for
 drizzling
– salt

Put the tomatoes into a heatproof bowl, cover with boiling water, and let stand for 1 minute before draining, then peel off the skins. Pat them dry and slice them about ¼ inch/ 5 mm thick. Sprinkle with salt and let drain.

Meanwhile, preheat the oven to 400°F/200°C/Gas Mark 6. Roll out the pastry dough and use it to line a 9-inch/ 23-cm shallow baking pan. Trim off any overlap and prick the bottom with a fork. Chill for about 30 minutes. Cover with parchment (baking) paper and fill with some pie weights (baking beans). Bake until firm, for about 20 minutes. Remove the paper and weights.

Spread the mustard over the bottom of the pastry shell and sprinkle the cheese evenly over the mustard. Arrange the tomatoes, slightly overlapping, over the cheese, and sprinkle with the herbes de Provence, followed by a little olive oil. Bake the tart for about 20 minutes, them remove and serve hot.

RUSTICA ALLO SPECK

CHEESE AND SPECK PIE

AVERAGE

– Preparation time: *20 minutes*
  + 30 minutes chilling
– Cooking time: *30 minutes*
– Calories per portion: *620*
– *Serves 6*

INGREDIENTS

– scant 1 cup (7 oz/200 g)
  robiola or cream cheese
– 3½ oz/100 g speck (smoked
  prosciutto), finely chopped
– 3½ oz/100 g fontina cheese,
  diced
– 2 eggs, lightly beaten, plus
  1 egg yolk, beaten with
  a little water
– 11 oz/300 g Basic Pie Dough
  (Shortcrust Pastry), see
  page 15
– all-purpose (plain) flour, for
  dusting
– 10 fresh basil leaves, finely
  chopped
– salt

Preheat the oven to 375°F/190°C/Gas Mark 5 and line a 10-inch/25-cm tart pan with parchment (baking) paper. Mix the robiola cheese in a bowl with the speck, fontina cheese, and whole eggs and set aside.

Roll out two-thirds of the pastry dough into a disk on a lightly floured surface, sprinkle with the chopped basil, and roll again with the rolling pin so that the dough is flecked with the green basil.

Use the dough to line the tart pan and place in the refrigerator to chill about 30 minutes, until firm.

Cover the dough with parchment (baking) paper and fill with some pie weights (baking beans). Bake for about 20 minutes. Remove the paper weights and reduce the temperature to 325°F/160°C/Gas Mark 3.

Spoon in the filling. Roll the remaining dough thinly on a lightly floured surface, cut it into strips, and weave a lattice on top of the filling. Brush the pastry strips with egg yolk.

Bake for 25–30 minutes. Let cool for a few minutes before transferring to a serving dish. Serve.

Tip: Never chop basil with a metal knife, as this causes the leaves to oxidize and turn black. Use a ceramic knife or tear the leaves into very small pieces.

TORTA DI RICOTTA, SALVIA, E PATATA DOLCE
RICOTTA, SAGE, AND SWEET POTATO TART

AVERAGE

– Preparation time: *25 minutes*
– Cooking time: *25–30 minutes*
– Calories per serving: *415*
– *Serves 8*

INGREDIENTS

– olive oil, for brushing
– 4½ cups (2¼ lb/1 kg) ricotta cheese
– 2⅓ cups (7 oz/200 g) grated Parmesan cheese
– 2 eggs
– 3½ cups (100 g/3½ oz) arugula (rocket)
– 2 tablespoons chopped fresh flat-leaf parsley
– 2 oz/50 g fresh sage leaves
– olive oil
– 1 sweet potato, thinly sliced
– 2½ tablespoons (1¼ oz/ 30 g) butter
– salt and pepper

Preheat the oven to 325°F/160°C/Gas Mark 3 and brush a square 9½-inch/24-cm baking pan with oil. Put the ricotta, Parmesan, and eggs into a food processor and process. Add the arugula (rocket), parsley, and half the sage leaves and process again.

Pour the cheese mixture into the baking pan, arrange the sweet potato on top, season with salt and pepper, and drizzle over a little oil. Bake for 20–25 minutes.

Meanwhile, melt the butter in a small saucepan over low heat and cook the remaining sage leaves. Remove the tart, sprinkle it with the buttered sage leaves, and let cool until just warm. Serve at room temperature.

Tip: The tart can be prepared in advance. Just before serving, cover it with a sheet of aluminum foil and heat it over a saucepan of boiling water. Add the sage-flavored butter.

TORTINI DI FUNGHI CHIODINI ALLA FONTINA

MUSHROOM AND CHEESE TARTLETS

EASY

– Preparation time: *1 hour
+ 24 hours chilling*
– Cooking time: *40 minutes*
– Calories per portion: *431*
– *Serves 6*

FOR THE PIE DOUGH (SHORTCRUST PASTRY)

– 2 cups (9 oz/250 g)
all-purpose (plain) flour
– 1½ sticks (6 oz/175 g) butter
– 1 egg, lightly beaten
– salt

FOR THE FILLING

– 4 eggs, plus 2 egg yolks
– ⅔ cup (5 fl oz/150 ml) milk
– scant ½ cup (3½ fl oz/
100 ml) light (single) cream
– 1¼ cups (3½ oz/100 g)
grated Parmesan cheese
– 2 lb 10 oz/1.2 kg
mixed wild mushrooms
– 3 bay leaves
– scant ½ cup (3½ fl oz/
100 ml) dry white wine
– 2½ tablespoons (1¼ oz/
30 g) butter
– 1 shallot, finely chopped
– sprig of fresh flat-leaf
parsley, chopped
– 5 oz/150 g fontina cheese,
sliced
– salt and pepper

Sift the flour into a mound on a clean work surface, make a well in the center, and add the butter. Rub the butter into the flour with your fingertips until it resembles bread crumbs. Work quickly to avoid heating the mixture too much. Add the egg, a pinch of salt, and ½ cup (4 fl oz/120 ml) cold water, bring it together to form a dough, shape it into a ball, and wrap it in plastic wrap (clingfilm). Let chill in the refrigerator for 24 hours.

Preheat the oven to 400°F/200°C/Gas Mark 6. Roll the dough out to a thickness of ⅛ inch/3 mm and use it to line a 10-inch/25-cm baking pan or 4-inch/10-cm individual molds. Cover the dough with aluminum foil, put pie weights (baking beans) inside each, and bake for about 10 minutes. Remove from the oven and reduce the oven temperature to 375°F/190°C/Gas Mark 5. Remove the foil and weights.

In a heavy saucepan, combined the whole eggs, egg yolks, milk, cream, and Parmesan, and season with salt and pepper. Cook over low heat, whisking continuously. When the mixture is creamy, transfer to a bowl and let cool.

Bring a large saucepan of salted water to a boil, add the mushrooms, bay leaves, and white wine, and cook for a few minutes, then drain. Melt the butter in a small saucepan, add the shallot, and cook gently, then add the mushrooms. Season with salt and pepper. When they have colored, sprinkle with the chopped parsley. Pour the cooled egg mixture into the cooked pastry shell (case). Place the mushrooms on top and cover with the sliced fontina cheese. Bake for 40 minutes, or until golden brown, then remove and serve.

SCHIACCIATA
CON BROCCOLETTI
BROCCOLI PIE

EASY

– Preparation time: *40 minutes*
  + 30 minutes resting
– Cooking time: *45 minutes*
– Calories per serving: *534*
– *Serves 6*

INGREDIENTS

– 3 cups (1 lb/450 g)
  all-purpose (plain) flour
– ⅔ cup (5 fl oz/150 ml) oil,
  plus extra for frying and
  brushing
– 1 clove garlic, crushed
– 2 cups (7 oz/170 g) broccoli,
  finely chopped
– 3 oz/80 g pecorino cheese,
  cut into slivers
– salt and pepper

Preheat the oven to 375°F/190°C/Gas Mark 5 and brush a baking sheet with oil. Sift the flour into a large bowl, make a well in the center, and add the oil and ¼ cup (2 fl oz/60 ml) water. Mix with your hands to form a firm and elastic dough. Divide into 2 disks, one slightly larger than the other, cover with plastic wrap (clingfilm), and let rest for about 30 minutes.

Heat 2 tablespoons oil in a large skillet or frying pan, add the garlic, and cook until lightly browned, then discard. Stir in the broccoli and cook for a few minutes, then drizzle in 3 tablespoons water, season with salt and pepper, and cook for about 6–8 minutes, or until the liquid has evaporated and the broccoli is tender but still firm to the bite.

Divide the dough in half and roll it out into 2 thin disks on a lightly floured work surface. Place one of the disks on the prepared baking sheet. Place the broccoli on top, leaving a 1-inch/2.5-cm border around the edge. Sprinkle the broccoli with the cheese.

Place the other disk on top and press down well around the edges to seal the pie, then prick it with a fork and brush it with oil. Bake for 30 minutes, then remove from the oven and serve hot.

CROSTATA DI ZUCCHINE, PROSCIUTTO, E RICOTTA

ZUCCHINI, HAM, AND RICOTTA CHEESE TART

AVERAGE

– Preparation time: *20 minutes*
– Cooking time: *50 minutes–
  1 hour*
– Calories per serving: *404*
– *Serves 6*

INGREDIENTS

– ¾ quantity Basic Pie Dough
  (Shortcrust Pastry), see
  page 105
– 2 tablespoons olive oil
– 1 small onion, finely
  chopped
– 3 zucchini (courgettes),
  sliced into thin rounds
– 3 eggs, plus 2 egg yolks
– ⅔ cup (5 oz/150 g) ricotta
  cheese
– 7 oz/200 g ham, finely
  chopped
– ⅔ cup (2 oz/50 g)
  grated Parmesan cheese
– pinch of freshly grated
  nutmeg
– salt and pepper

Preheat the oven to 375°F/190°C/Gas Mark 5 and line
a baking sheet with parchment (baking) paper. Roll out
the pastry dough into a 11-inch/28-cm disk on the lined
baking sheet. Chill in the refrigerator while making
the filling.

Heat the oil in a skillet or frying pan over medium heat,
add the onion, and cook gently for 5 minutes, then add
the zucchini (courgettes), cover the pan, and cook for
5–10 minutes, or until translucent and lightly browned.
Once cooked, remove the lid, increase the heat, and
continue cooking until all the liquid has evaporated.
Transfer to a plate and set aside to cool slightly.

Meanwhile, whisk the whole eggs with 1 egg yolk
in a large bowl, add the ricotta, and mix well. Add
the ham, Parmesan, and nutmeg. Stir and season
with salt and pepper.

Arrange the cheese filling on top of the dough, without
squashing it too much and leaving a 2-inch/5-cm border,
then cover with a single layer of the zucchini. Fold over
the edges of the dough. Beat the remaining egg yolk with
a little water and use it to brush the edges of the dough.
Bake for 40–45 minutes, remove, and let stand for a few
minutes. Transfer to a serving dish and serve hot
or at room temperature.

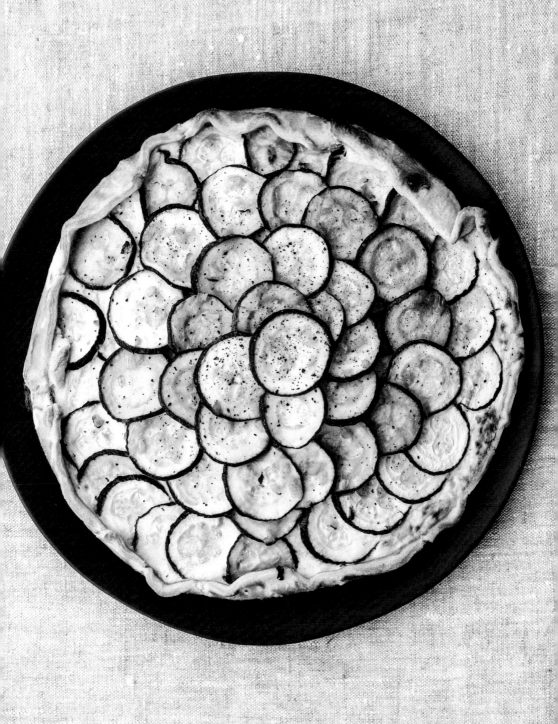

TORTA DI FINOCCHI

FENNEL PIE

EASY

– Preparation time: *30*
– Cooking time: *50 minutes*
– Calories per serving: *652*
– *Serves 6*

INGREDIENTS

– 7 tablespoons (3 ½ oz/100 g) butter, plus extra for greasing
– 6 fennel bulbs, chopped
– 1 lb 2 oz/500 g ready-to-bake puff pastry, thawed if frozen
– all-purpose (plain) flour, for dusting
– 7 oz/200 g Taleggio cheese, sliced
– 3 eggs plus 1 egg yolk
– ¾ cup (6 fl oz/175 ml) milk
– salt and pepper

Preheat the oven to 350°F/180°C/Gas Mark 4 and grease a large pie dish with butter. Melt the butter in a large saucepan, add the fennel, and cook over medium-low heat, stirring occasionally, for 8–10 minutes, until softened.

Roll out two-thirds of the dough on a lightly floured surface and line the pie dish with the dough. Trim the edges and brush the rim with water. Spoon the fennel into the dish and top with the slices of cheese.

Beat together the whole eggs and milk in a bowl, season with salt and pepper, and pour the mixture over the fennel and cheese. Roll out the remaining dough, place it over the pie, and press the edges to seal. Brush the surface with beaten egg yolk and bake for about 40 minutes, until golden brown.

CROSTATA AL FORMAGGIO

RUSTIC BREAD TART

EASY

– Preparation time: *30 minutes*
– Cooking time: *40 minutes*
– Calories per serving: *811–540*
– *Serves 4–6*

INGREDIENTS

– butter, for greasing
– 2 eggs
– 1½ cups (4 oz/120 g) grated
– Parmesan cheese
– 6 tablespoons olive oil
– pinch of grated lemon zest
– 2 cups (16 fl oz/475 ml) milk
– 4 cups (7 oz/200 g) grated
  bread or coarse fresh
  bread crumbs
– 1 cup (8 fl oz/250 ml) light
  (single) cream
– sliced salami, to serve
– salt

Preheat the oven to 350°F/180°C/Gas Mark 4 and grease a 10½-inch/28-cm baking pan or line it with parchment (baking) paper. Beat the eggs in a bowl with 1¼ cups (3½ oz/100 g) grated Parmesan, 4 tablespoons oil, grated lemon zest, and a pinch of salt.

Gradually stir in the milk and add the bread crumbs and cream to the mixture. Pour it into the prepared pan and pour in the remaining oil.

Bake for about 40 minutes. When the tart has 5 minutes left to cook, sprinkle it with the remaining grated Parmesan. Remove from the oven and serve warm with small slices of salami.

TORTA ALLE ERBE PROFUMATE
FRESH CHEESE AND MIXED HERB TART

EASY

- Preparation time: *15 minutes
  + 30 minutes chilling*
- Cooking time: *30 minutes*
- Calories per serving: *705*
- *Serves 4–6*

INGREDIENTS

- generous ¾ quantity Basic
  Pie Dough (Shortcrust
  Pastry), see page 105
- all-purpose (plain) flour,
  for dusting
- 3 eggs plus 1 egg yolk
- 2 small goat cheeses
- 2 (1 oz/30 g) Petit Suisse or
  ¼ cup (2 oz/50 g)cream
  cheese
- 1 cup (8 fl oz/250 ml) light
  (single) cream
- 1½ cups (2½ oz/60 g) mixed
  fresh herbs, such as chives,
  tarragon, parsley, and
  chervil, chopped
- salt and pepper

Preheat the oven to 400°F/200°C/Gas Mark 6 and line a 10-inch/25-cm baking pan with parchment (baking) paper.

Roll out the dough into a disk on a lightly floured surface, use it to line the baking pan, and prick the dough with a fork. Let chill in the refrigerator, for about 30 minutes.

To make the filling, beat the whole eggs and egg yolk with the cheeses and cream in a bowl, add the chopped herbs, and season with salt and pepper.

Take the pastry shell (case) out of the refrigerator, pour the filling into it, and bake for 15 minutes before reducing the temperature to 375°F/190°C/Gas Mark 5 for another 15 minutes. Remove from the oven and let stand for 2 minutes, then transfer it to a serving dish and serve immediately.

Tip: Chop the tarragon, parsley, and chervil leaves finely with a knife, but snip the chives with kitchen scissors or cut with an extremely sharp knife to avoid crushing them.

CROSTATA DI ZUCCHINE

ZUCCHINI TART

EASY

- Preparation time: *20 minutes*
- Cooking time: *55 minutes*
- Calories per serving: *420*
- *Serves 6*

INGREDIENTS

- ¼ cup (1¼ oz/30 g) pine nuts
- 4–5 tablespoons extra virgin olive oil
- 1 clove garlic, crushed
- 1¾ lb/800 g zucchini (courgettes), peeled and coarsely grated
- small bunch fresh basil, chopped
- scant 1 cup (7 fl oz/200 ml) light (single) cream
- 2 eggs, lightly beaten
- 1 cup (3 oz/80 g) grated Parmesan cheese
- 8 oz/240 g ready-to-bake puff pastry
- 2 tablespoons bread crumbs
- salt

Preheat the oven to 350°F/180°C/Gas Mark 4 and line a deep 8½-inch/22-cm baking pan with parchment (baking) paper. Soak the pine nuts in a bowl of cold water for 20 minutes. Drain, dry them, and set aside.

Heat the oil in a saucepan, add the crushed garlic and cook gently. Discard the garlic, add the zucchini (courgettes), season with salt, and cook over high heat for 10–15 minutes, until their liquid has evaporated. Cool, season with salt, and add the basil leaves, cream, eggs, and Parmesan. Stir well.

Roll out the pastry and use it to line the prepared pan. Sprinkle bread crumbs over the bottom of the pastry and pour the zucchini (courgette) mixture on top. Sprinkle the pine nuts over the surface and bake on the bottom shelf for about 40 minutes. Serve warm or cold.

CROSTATA ALLA TREVIGIANA

TREVISO-STYLE TART

EASY

– Preparation time: *30 minutes
  + 30 minutes chilling*
– Cooking time: *10 minutes*
– Calories per portion: *616*
– *Serves 6*

INGREDIENTS

– 3 tablespoons olive oil
– 2 shallots, finely chopped
– 2 heads radicchio (chicory),
  coarsely chopped
– 1 lb/450 g Basic Pie Dough
  (Shortcrust Pastry),
  see page 105
– 7 oz/200 g fresh pork
  sausages
– ¼ cup (2 fl oz/50 ml) dry
  white wine
– 7 oz/200 g fontina cheese,
  diced
– 2 eggs
– scant ½ cup
  (3½ fl oz/100 ml) light
  (single) cream
– salt and pepper

Line a 10-inch/25-cm round baking pan with parchment (baking) paper. Heat the oil in a skillet or frying pan, add the shallots, radicchio (chicory), and 2 tablespoons water and cook for 2–3 minutes over high heat. Season with a pinch of salt.

Roll out the dough on a lightly floured surface to a thickness of ⅛ inch/3 mm and use it to line the baking pan. Prick the bottom with a fork and chill in the refrigerator for 30 minutes.

Preheat the oven to 375°F/190°C/Gas Mark 5. Cover the dough with parchment (baking) paper and fill with pie weights (baking beans). Bake for about 20 minutes. Reduce the temperature to 325°F/160°C/Gas Mark 3 and remove the paper and weights.

Cook the sausages in the wine, diluted with a little water, for 3 minutes. Remove and let cool, then skin and crumble the sausage meat.

Spread out the sausage meat in the pastry shell (case), followed the fontina cheese. Beat the eggs with the cream, season with salt and pepper, and pour them over the sausage and cheese. Bake for about 25 minutes, then transfer to a serving dish and serve.

TORTA ALLA RUCOLA E TALEGGIO

ARUGULA AND TALEGGIO PIE

AVERAGE

– Preparation time: *15 minutes*
+ 1 hour resting
– Cooking time: *1 hour*
– Calories per serving: *592*
– *Serves 6*

FOR THE DOUGH

– 1¾ cups (8 oz/225 g)
all-purpose (plain) flour,
plus extra for dusting
– 1 tablespoon poppy seeds
– 1 tablespoon chopped
marjoram
– 7 tablespoons (3½ oz/100 g)
butter, chilled and diced,
plus extra for greasing

FOR THE FILLING

– 1½ cups arugula (rocket)
– 1⅓ cups (11 oz/200 g)
cream cheese
– 7 oz/200 g Taleggio cheese,
diced
– 2 tablespoons bread crumbs
– 2 eggs
– salt and pepper

Sift the flour with a pinch of salt into a mound in a large bowl or on a work surface, sprinkle with the poppy seeds and marjoram, and rub in the butter with your fingertips. Add enough cold water to make a soft dough, then shape into a ball, cover with plastic wrap (clingfilm), and let rest for 1 hour.

Preheat the oven to 375°F/190°C/Gas Mark 4. Grease an 8-inch/20-cm tart pan with butter. Parboil the arugula (rocket) for a few minutes in salted water, then drain, squeezing out as much liquid as possible. In a food processor, combine the arugula, both cheeses, the bread crumbs, and eggs. Process at low speed, then season with salt and pepper.

Roll out the dough on a lightly floured surface, and line the prepared pan. Trim the edges and reserve the scraps. Cover with parchment (baking) paper and fill with some pie weights (baking beans). Bake for about 20 minutes. Reduce the temperature to 325°F/160°C/Gas Mark 3.

Remove the weights and fill the pastry shell (case) with the arugula and cheese mixture. Roll out the scraps, cut into thin strips, brush the ends with water, and arrange in a lattice over the top of the pie. Bake for about 40 minutes.

ERBAZZONE

SAVORY PIE

EASY

– Preparation time: *30 minutes*
– Cooking time: *55 minutes*
– Calories per serving: *398*
– *Serves 6*

INGREDIENTS

– 3¼ lb/1.5 kg catalogna
  chicory or curly (frisse)
  lettuce
– 2 shallots, thinly sliced
– 2 cloves garlic
– ¾ quantity Basic Bread
  Dough (see page 15)
– all-purpose (plain) flour, for
  dusting
– 2 tablespoons olive oil, plus
  extra for greasing
  and drizzling
– 1 cup (3 oz/80 g) grated
  Parmesan cheese
– salt and pepper

Preheat the oven to 400°F/200°C/Gas Mark 6 and grease a baking sheet. Bring a saucepan of water to a boil, add the catalogna chicory, and cook for 5–6 minutes, then drain and cut into pieces. Heat the oil in a saucepan, add the shallots, season with pepper, and cook gently. When they start to color, add the chicory and garlic and season with salt and pepper. Continue cooking for about 20 minutes.

Roll out the dough into 2 disks on a lightly floured surface. Place a disk on the baking sheet and spread the cooked vegetables on top, then sprinkle with the Parmesan and some pepper. Cover with the second disk and pinch the edges together to seal. Prick the top with a fork and brush with oil.

Bake for 25 minutes, then remove from the oven and let stand for 5 minutes before serving.

TORTA AL CAVOLFIORE

CAULIFLOWER TART

EASY

– Preparation time: *20 minutes*
– Cooking time: *45 minutes*
– Calories per serving: *530*
– *Serves 4*

INGREDIENTS

– 1 cauliflower, cut into florets
– 13 oz/375 g ready-to-bake
  puff pastry
– 1½ tablespoons milk
– 4 eggs, lightly beaten
– pinch of freshly grated
  nutmeg
– generous ¾ cup
  (3½ oz/100 g) grated
  Emmental cheese
– salt and pepper

Preheat the oven to 400°F/200°C/Gas Mark 6. Bring a large saucepan of salted water to a boil, add the cauliflower florets, and cook for 10 minutes, then drain and let cool.

Roll out the puff pastry into an 8 x 10-inch/20 x 25-cm rectangle on a lightly floured surface, place it on a baking sheet, and bake for 5–10 minutes. Remove from the oven and arrange the cauliflower florets on top. Reduce the oven temperature to 320°F/160°C/ Gas Mark 3.

Mix the milk, eggs, nutmeg, and cheese in a bowl and season with salt and pepper. Stir well and pour this mixture over the cauliflower florets, then bake for about 25 minutes. Remove from the oven and let cool, then slice it and serve.

Tip: To prevent the cauliflower from releasing too much water during cooking, you can steam it instead. Divide it into small florets, place in a steamer, and cook for about 10 minutes, or until tender.

CROSTATA AI PEPERONI

BELL PEPPER TART

AVERAGE

– Preparation time: *25 minutes*
– Cooking time: *30–35 minutes*
– Calories per serving: *625*
– *Serves 6*

INGREDIENTS

– 1⅓ quantities Basic Pie Dough (Shortcrust Pastry), see page 105
– 2½ tablespoons (1¼ oz/30 g) butter
– 1 shallot, finely chopped
– 3–4 red bell peppers, seeded and diced
– 3½ oz/100 g provolone cheese
– 3 eggs
– scant 1 cup (7 fl oz/200 ml) heavy (double) cream
– salt and pepper

Preheat the oven to 375°F/190°C/Gas Mark 5 and line a shallow 8 x 10-inch/20 x 25-cm baking pan with parchment (baking) paper. Roll out the dough thinly on a lightly floured surface and use to line the bottom and sides of a baking pan. Trim away the excess and chill for 30 minutes. Line with aluminum foil, fill with pie weights (baking beans), and bake for 20 minutes. Remove the foil and weights, prick the bottom with a fork, and bake for another 5–10 minutes.

Meanwhile, melt the butter in a saucepan, add the shallot and bell peppers, season with salt, cover, and cook for 7–8 minutes, or until the peppers are soft. While the peppers are cooking, cut the provolone cheese into little strips. Beat the eggs in a bowl and add the cream, provolone cheese, and cooked peppers. Season with salt and pepper.

Pour the mixture into the baking pan and bake for 25 minutes. Remove and let stand for few minutes, then transfer to a serving dish. Serve hot or warm.

TORTA SALATA CON PORRI E PROSCIUTTO

HAM AND LEEK TART

EASY

– Preparation time: *30 minutes*
– Cooking time: *45 minutes*
– Calories per serving: *605*
– *Serves 8–10*

INGREDIENTS

– 14 oz/400 g ready-to-bake puff pastry
– 2 tablespoons olive oil
– 6 leeks, thinly sliced
– 4 eggs
– scant ½ cup (3½ fl oz/ 100 ml) light (single) cream
– ¾ cup (2½ oz/60 g) grated Parmesan cheese
– 2½ oz/60 g ham, chopped
– sprig of fresh flat-leaf parsley, chopped
– salt

Preheat the oven to 425°F/200°C/Gas Mark 6. Roll out the pastry on a lightly floured surface into a thin disk and use it to line a deep 9-inch/23-cm springform pan. Reserve any pastry scraps for decoration. Cover the pastry with a sheet of aluminum foil, put pie weights (baking beans) inside it, and bake for about 15 minutes. Remove the paper and weights. Reduce the oven to 350°F/180°C/Gas Mark 4 and bake for another 5 minutes.

Heat the oil in a skillet or frying pan, add the leeks, sprinkle them with 3 tablespoons of water, and cook gently for 15 minutes. Remove from the heat and let cool.

Beat the eggs with the cream in a bowl and add the grated Parmesan and a pinch of salt. Stir in the leeks, ham, and parsley. Mix well and pour into the shell (case). Fold over the edges of the pastry toward the center. Cut out leaf shapes from the pastry scraps and arrange these on top of the tart. Bake for 25 minutes, then remove and let stand for a few minutes before serving.

Tip: If using a convection (fan) oven, cook the pastry on the bottom shelf—it takes more heat from below and the bottom will cook evenly, even if in contact with a moist filling.

TORTA DI BIETOLINE E RICOTTA

SWISS CHARD AND RICOTTA PIE

EASY

– Preparation time: *20 minutes*
  + 30 minutes chilling
– Cooking time: *35 minutes*
– Calories per portion: *360*
– *Serves 8*

FOR THE PIE DOUGH
(SHORTCRUST PASTRY)

– 4¼ cups (1 lb 2 oz/500 g)
  all-purpose (plain) flour,
  plus extra for dusting
– 2 tablespoons olive oil, plus
  extra for brushing
– ½ teaspoon salt

FOR THE FILLING

– 1 lb 6 oz/625 g baby Swiss
  chard or baby spinach
– generous 1 cup (9 oz/250 g)
  ricotta cheese
– 1½ cups (4½ oz/120 g)
  grated Parmesan cheese
– 1 onion, finely chopped
– 1 egg, lightly beaten
– salt and pepper

Soak the baby Swiss chard or spinach in a bowl of salted water for 30 minutes.

To make the dough, sift the flour into a bowl, make a well in the center, and add the oil, salt, and 1 cup (8 fl oz/250 ml) water. Bring it together with your hands to form a dough, then shape it into a ball and wrap it in plastic wrap (clingfilm). Chill in the refrigerator for 30 minutes.

Preheat the oven to 350°F/180°C/Gas Mark 4 and line an 8 x 12-inch/20 x 30-cm baking pan with parchment (baking) paper. On a lightly floured surface, roll the dough out thinly into two 10 x 14-inches/25 x 35-cm rectangles, and use one of these to line the baking pan.

To make the filling, drain and squeeze the chard or spinach thoroughly, chop coarsely, mix it with the ricotta, Parmesan, onion, and egg, and season with salt and pepper. Spread out this filling in the baking pan and cover with the remaining rectangle of dough.

Brush generously with olive oil. Bake for about 35 minutes. Take out of the oven, rest it for 5 minutes, then serve.

TORTA CON VERDURE MISTE E MOZZARELLA

VEGETABLE AND MOZZARELLA PIE

AVERAGE

– Preparation time: *20 minutes + 30 minutes chilling*
– Cooking time: *35 minutes*
– Calories per serving: *618*
– *Serves 4*

INGREDIENTS

– 3 tablespoons olive oil, plus extra for drizzling
– 2 small, long eggplants (aubergines), cubed
– 3 zucchini (courgettes), sliced
– 2 scallions (spring onions), sliced thinly
– 9 oz/250 g ready-to-bake puff pastry
– 7 oz/200 g mozzarella cheese, cubed
– salt and pepper

Preheat the oven to 425°F/220°C/Gas Mark 7. Heat the oil in a skillet or frying pan and add the eggplants (aubergines) and zucchini (courgettes). Cook for about 10 minutes. Add the scallions (spring onions) to the pan, cook for another 5 minutes, and season with salt and pepper.

Roll out the pastry to a disk shape on a lightly floured work surface and use it to line a round 10-inch/25-cm springform baking pan. Press the sides and the base down and trim off any overlap. Chill in the refrigerator until firm, about 30 minutes.

Prick with a fork, arrange the mixed vegetables on top, and drizzle with a little oil. Sprinkle the mozzarella over the top. Bake for 20 minutes. Remove from the oven and let stand for 2 minutes, then transfer to a serving dish. Serve.

Tip: For a softer and more delicate filling, peel the eggplants before they are diced.

TORTA CON PORRI E TALEGGIO
LEEK AND TALEGGIO TART

INGREDIENTS

- generous ¾ quantity Basic Pie Dough (Shortcrust Pastry), see page 105
- all-purpose (plain) flour, for dusting
- 5 tablespoons (2½ oz/60 g) butter
- 14 oz/400 g leeks, white and pale green parts only, thinly sliced
- 1 egg, plus 1 egg yolk
- ½ cup (4 fl oz/120 ml) heavy (double) cream
- ⅔ cup (50 g/2 oz) grated Parmesan cheese
- 5 oz/150 g Taleggio, diced
- salt and pepper

Preheat the oven to 375°F/190°C/Gas Mark 5 and place a baking sheet on the middle shelf of the oven. Roll out the pastry dough on a lightly floured surface into a disk large enough to line the bottom and sides of a 9-inch/23-cm tart pan. Chill the pastry shell (case) in the refrigerator for about 30 minutes, until firm.

To make the filling, melt the butter in a large saucepan, add the leeks, cover, and cook for 10 minutes over medium heat, then remove the lid and cook for over medium-low heat for another 5 minutes until tender. Stir occasionally. Remove from the heat and transfer to a plate to cool.

In a bowl, whisk together the egg, egg yolk, cream, and Parmesan and season a little salt and pepper.

Cover with parchment (baking) paper and fill with some pie weights (baking beans). Bake for about 20 minutes. Reduce the heat to 325°F/160°C/Gas Mark 3 and bake for 25 minutes. Remove the paper and weights.

Spread the leeks out in the pastry case, sprinkle with the diced Taleggio, and pour the egg and cream mixture over them. Remove from the oven and let stand for a few minutes before transferring it to a serving dish. Serve warm or at room temperature.

TORTA DI BRESAOLA

BRESAOLA TART

EASY

– Preparation time: *30 minutes*
– Cooking time: *50 minutes*
– Calories per serving: *494*
– *Serves 6*

INGREDIENTS

– butter, for greasing
– flour, for dusting
– 11 oz/300 g ready-to-bake
  puff pastry
– 3 tablespoons olive oil
– 1 clove garlic, crushed
– 2 zucchini (courgettes),
  sliced
– sprig of fresh flat-leaf parsley,
  chopped
– 2 eggs
– scant ½ cup (3½ oz/100 g)
  light (single) cream
– 3 tablespoons fresh bread
  crumbs
– 5 oz/150 g bresaola, chopped
– 1 tablespoon pine nuts
– salt and pepper

Preheat the oven to 350°F/180°C/Gas Mark 4 and grease and dust a 9-inch/23-cm baking pan. Roll out the pastry on a lightly floured surface and use it to line the baking pan up to the edges. Cover with parchment (baking) paper and fill with some pie weights (baking beans). Bake for about 20 minutes, then remove the paper and weights.

Heat 2 tablespoons oil in a skillet or frying pan, add the garlic, and cook gently until golden, then discard it and add the zucchini (courgettes). Cook for 15 minutes. Remove from the heat and sprinkle with the parsley. Beat the eggs and cream in a bowl and season with salt and pepper. Heat the remaining oil in a skillet or frying pan, add the bread crumbs, and cook lightly until golden.

Remove the baking beans and parchment (baking) paper from the pastry case and sprinkle the bread crumbs over the pastry shell (case). Arrange alternate layers of bresaola, zucchini, and pine nuts on top. Pour over the egg and cream mixture and bake for 20 minutes.

CROSTATA AL SALMONE
E PORRI

SALMON AND LEEK TART

AVERAGE

– Preparation time: *40 minutes*
  + 30 minutes chilling
– Cooking time: *35 minutes*
– Calories per serving: *614*
– *Serves 4*

FOR THE PASTRY

– 7 tablespoons (3½ oz/100 g)
  butter, softened
– 1⅔ cups (7 oz/200 g)
  all-purpose (plain) flour

FOR THE FILLING

– 3 eggs
– scant 1 cup (7 fl oz/
  200 ml) milk
– pinch of freshly grated
  nutmeg
– 2 tablespoons olive oil
– 1 leek, white part only, sliced
– 3½ oz/100 g smoked salmon,
  finely chopped
– salt and freshly ground white
  pepper
– mixed salad greens (leaves),
  to serve

Put the butter into a bowl, sift in the flour, and mix them together with your hands to make a smooth and compact dough. Chill in the refrigerator for 30 minutes.

Preheat the oven to 350°F/180°C/Gas Mark 4. Roll out the dough to a thin sheet on a lightly floured surface and use it to line an 8-inch/20-cm baking pan. Cover with parchment (baking) paper and fill with some pie weights (baking beans). Bake for about 20 minutes, then remove the paper and weights.

Beat the eggs with the milk in a bowl and add a pinch of nutmeg. Season with salt and pepper and set aside.

Heat the oil in a skillet or frying pan, add the leek, and cook gently for 10 minutes. Season with salt and pepper and remove from the heat. Let cool, then spread over the pastry shell (case). Sprinkle the smoked salmon on top and pour over the beaten eggs. Bake for about 25 minutes. Remove, let cool, and then serve with a green salad.

Tip: Leeks can contain traces of soil in their leaves. To clean a leek thoroughly, remove the green part, cut a deep cross in it on the opposite side to the root and rinse several times under running water.

TORTA DI VERDURE
CON PROSCIUTTO CRUDO
VEGETABLE AND PROSCIUTTO PIE

EASY

– Preparation time: *30 minutes*
  + 1 hour chilling
– Cooking time: *1 hour*
– Calories per portion: *485*
– *Serves 8*

FOR THE PASTRY

– 2½ cups (11 oz/300 g)
  all-purpose (plain) flour,
  plus extra for dusting
– 7 tablespoons (3½ oz/100 g)
  butter, cubed, plus extra for
  greasing
– ⅓ cup (3 fl oz/75 ml) cold
  milk
– pinch of salt

FOR THE FILLING

– 7 oz/200 g mozzarella
  cheese, thinly sliced
– 5 oz/150 g prosciutto (Parma
  Ham), fat removed and
  thinly sliced
– ½ cup (2 oz/60 g) Taleggio
  cheese, grated
– 2 cups (11 oz/300 g) cooked
  spinach, squeezed dry and
  chopped
– 1 cup (5 oz/150 g) cooked
  peas
– 2 eggs, lightly beaten, plus
  1 egg yolk
– salt and pepper

Sift the flour with a pinch of salt into a large bowl
and add the butter. Rub in with your fingertips until
the mixture resembles bread crumbs. Make a well
in the center and pour in the cold milk, or enough to
make a smooth and homogeneous mixture, and bring
together to form a dough. Shape the dough into a ball,
wrap in plastic wrap (clingfilm), and refrigerate for at
least 1 hour.

Preheat the oven to 350°F/180°C/Gas Mark 4 and grease
and dust a 10½-inch/28-cm baking pan. Roll out just
over half the dough into a disk on a lightly floured
surface and use it to line the baking pan. Prick the
bottom with a fork.

Arrange a layer of half mozzarella cheese on the dough,
followed by a layer of prosciutto (Parma ham), then the
remaining mozzarella. Sprinkle with 2–3 tablespoons
grated cheese and a little pepper between each layer.
Make a final layer with the spinach and peas. Pour the
beaten eggs on top and sprinkle with 4 tablespoons
grated cheese. Season with salt and pepper.

Roll out the remaining dough into a disk, use it to cover
the pie, and seal the edges well. Beat the egg yolk with
1 tablespoon water. Prick the top of the pastry and brush
it with the egg yolk. Bake for about 1 hour.

*Tip: Before you use the mozzarella, place the slices on
several sheets of paper towels, cover them with more paper
towels, and press down gently to eliminate as much whey
as possible.*

TORTA DI RISO LIGURE

LIGURIAN RICE CAKE

AVERAGE

– Preparation time: *15 minutes + 30 minutes resting*
– Cooking time: *50 minutes*
– Calories per portion: *465–349*
– *Serves 6–8*

INGREDIENTS

– generous 2 cups (9 oz/250 g) all-purpose (plain) flour
– 2 tablespoons olive oil
– ½ teaspoon salt
– 4¼ cups (1¾ pints/1 liter) milk
– 1½ cups (11 oz/300 g) brown risotto rice
– 1½ cups (7 oz/200 g) stracchino or Taleggio cheese, chopped
– 3 tablespoons grated Parmesan cheese
– pinch of freshly grated nutmeg
– 2 eggs
– a few fresh thyme leaves, to garnish
– pepper

Sift the flour onto a clean work surface or into a large bowl, make a well in the center, and add ½ cup (4 fl oz/120 ml) lukewarm water, the oil, and the salt to taste. Bring together with your hands to form a soft and smooth dough. Wrap the dough in plastic wrap (clingfilm) and let rest for 30 minutes.

Bring the milk to boiling point with a pinch of salt, add the rice, and cook according to package directions. Drain the rice in a strainer (sieve) over a bowl, reserving the cooking liquid.

Preheat the oven to 375°F/190°C/Gas Mark 5 and line a 9½-inch/24-cm baking pan with parchment (baking) paper.

Place the rice in a large bowl and stir in ⅔ cup (5 fl oz/ 150 ml) reserved cooking milk, the stracchino cheese, and Parmesan, then season with salt and pepper and add a pinch of nutmeg. Beat the eggs and stir them into the rice mixture.

Roll out the dough thinly and line the bottom and sides the baking pan. Fill it with the rice mixture and fold the dough edges inward. Bake for 35–40 minutes, or until the center is set. Serve warm or cold, garnished with a few thyme leaves.

SFOGLIATA AI FUNGHI

MUSHROOM TART

EASY

– Preparation time: *20 minutes*
– Cooking time: *40–45 minutes*
– Calories per portion: *563*
– *Serves 4*

INGREDIENTS

– 8 oz/225 g ready-to-bake puff pastry
– all-purpose (plain) flour, for dusting
– 3 tablespoons olive oil
– 1 clove garlic, crushed
– 1 lb 2 oz/500 g mixed mushrooms
– 2 tablespoons chopped fresh chervil or parsley
– scant 1 cup (2 oz/50 g) fresh bread crumbs
– ⅔ cup (5 fl oz/150 ml) béchamel sauce
– ⅓ cup (1¼ oz/30 g) grated Parmesan cheese
– salt and pepper

Preheat the oven to 425°F/220°C/Gas Mark 7 and line a 9½-inch/24-cm tart pan with parchment (baking) paper. Roll out the pastry to a disk on a lightly floured surface, place it in the baking pan, and prick the bottom with a fork. Chill in the refrigerator while you make the filling.

Heat the oil in a skillet or frying pan, add the garlic clove and cook lightly before discarding it. Add the mushrooms and cook over medium-high heat for 15 minutes, or until dry and lightly browned. Season with salt and pepper, remove from the heat, and set aside. Place the chervil or tarragon in the food processor with the bread crumbs and process.

Meanwhile, gently heat the béchamel sauce in a small saucepan, stir in the Parmesan, and season with salt and pepper. Remove from the heat.

Take the pastry from the refrigerator and sprinkle with the bread crumb mixture, then spread out the mushrooms on top and pour in the béchamel sauce slowly to cover them. Bake for 20–25 minutes. Remove from the oven and transfer to a serving dish.

TORTA CAPOVOLTA AGRODOLCE DI PEPERONI E CIPOLLE

BELL PEPPER AND ONION TART

INGREDIENTS

– 2 red bell peppers, halved
  and seeds removed
– 2 yellow bell peppers, halved
  and seeds removed
– 1 large yellow onion, sliced
  ¼-inch/5 mm thick
– olive oil, for drizzling
– 1 tablespoon sugar
– 5 tablespoons white wine
  vinegar
– 10 fresh mint leaves,
  chopped
– 9 oz/250 g ready-to-bake
  puff pastry
– flour, for dusting
– salt and pepper

Preheat the oven to 400°F/200°C/Gas Mark 6. Line a large baking sheet with parchment (baking) paper and put the bell peppers on it. Add the onion, drizzle over with a little oil, and roast for about 10 minutes.

Set the onion aside. Place the peppers between 2 plates, let cool for about 10 minutes, then remove the skins and cut into thin strips. Reduce the oven temperature to 350°F/180°C/Gas Mark 4.

Dissolve the sugar in the vinegar and 2 tablespoons water in a nonstick flameproof 10½-inch/28-cm baking pan and cook over medium heat for a few minutes, stirring frequently, until it becomes a thick syrup.

Remove the baking pan from the heat and carefully tilt it so that the syrup coats the sides, then fill it with alternate layers of yellow and red bell peppers until it is completely covered. Season with salt and pepper, sprinkle with the chopped mint leaves, and place the onion slices on top of these. Season again.

Roll out the puff pastry into a thin disk on a lightly floured surface, place it over the bell peppers, and fold over the edges. Prick the surface with a fork and bake for 20–30 minutes, or until the top is golden brown. Unmold onto a serving dish and serve hot or warm.

TORTA CAPOVOLTA AI CARCIOFI

ARTICHOKE UPSIDE-DOWN TART

EASY

– Preparation time: *30 minutes*
– Cooking time: *1 hour*
– Calories per serving: *300*
– *Serves 6*

INGREDIENTS

– 2 tablespoons olive oil
– 1 clove garlic, finely chopped
– 3 tomatoes, diced
– 1 fennel bulb, diced
– 2 shallots, diced
– 6 artichoke bottoms
– 1–2 tablespoons olive tapenade
– 9 oz/250 g ready-to-bake puff pastry
– ⅔ cup (2 oz/50 g) grated Parmesan cheese
– salt and pepper

Preheat the oven to 350°F/180°C/Gas Mark 4. Heat the olive oil in a saucepan and add the garlic, tomatoes, fennel, and shallots. Season with salt and pepper and cook gently for 20 minutes. Cook the artichoke bottoms for 10 minutes in salted boiling water, until tender, then drain well.

Place the artichoke bottoms in a round mold or nonstick baking pan, leaving a small border around the edge. Sprinkle with the tapenade. Add the cooked vegetables and sprinkle with the grated Parmesan.

Roll out the puff pastry on a lightly floured surface into a thin disk slightly larger than the baking pan. Place the disk on top of the vegetables, tucking it in around them to enclose them.

Bake for about 30 minutes. Turn out onto a serving plate while still hot and serve upside-down.

STRUDELS

TECHNIQUE

TORTA ARROTOLATA CON RICOTTA, PEPERONI E OLIVE

RICOTTA, BELL PEPPER, AND OLIVE STRUDEL

AVERAGE

– Preparation time: *30 minutes
 + 1 hour resting*
– Cooking time: *45 minutes*
– Calories per portion: 483
– *Serves 6*

INGREDIENTS

– 1⅔ cups (7 oz/200 g)
 all-purpose (plain) flour
– 2 tablespoons extra virgin
 olive oil
– 2½ tablespoons (1¼ oz/30 g)
 butter
– 1 clove garlic, peeled
– ⅔ cup (1 oz/30 g) fresh
 bread crumbs
– 4 small sprigs fresh thyme,
 leaves chopped
– 1⅓ cups (11 oz/300 g)
 ricotta cheese
– 3 canned roasted red
 peppers, cut into thin strips
– 1 cup (4 oz/120 g) black
 pitted olives
– ¼ cup (¾ oz/20 g) grated
 pecorino romano cheese
– salt

STEP 1

Put the flour into a bowl, add a little salt, and the oil, drizzle in ½ cup (4 fl oz/120 ml) lukewarm water, and mix to a soft and smooth dough. Wrap the dough in plastic wrap (clingfilm) and let it rest for 1 hour. Preheat the oven to 425°F/220°C/Gas Mark 7. Melt two-thirds of the butter in a small saucepan, add the garlic, and cook gently, then add the bread crumbs and toast them, stirring frequently. Remove and discard the garlic and add the thyme.

STEP 2

Roll out the strudel dough on a lightly floured work surface, transfer it to a large sheet of parchment (baking) paper, and roll it out again until thin and almost transparent. Sprinkle with the aromatic bread crumbs, avoiding the edges.

STEP 3

Crumble the ricotta cheese over the dough, then the red peppers, olives, and pecorino cheese, leaving a border around the edges. Fold over the longer edges of the dough inward and, using the parchment (baking) paper underneath to help you, roll up the dough over the filling.

STEP 4

Bake for 45 minutes and serve warm.

TORTA ARROTOLATA DELL'ORTO

VEGETABLE STRUDEL

EASY

– Preparation time: *30 minutes*
– Cooking time: *1 hour*
– Calories per serving: *338*
– *Serves 8*

INGREDIENTS

– 6 tablespoons (3 oz/80 g)
  butter, plus 1 tablespoon,
  melted
– 1 clove garlic, crushed
– 2 cups (10 oz/300 g) peas,
  blanched
– 3 cups (10 oz/300 g) thin,
  young green beans, thinly
  sliced and blanched
– 10 oz/300 g asparagus, thinly
  sliced and blanched
– 10 oz/300 g artichoke hearts,
  thinly sliced and blanched
– 3 carrots, thinly
  sliced and blanched
– 7 oz/200 g new potatoes,
  thinly sliced and blanched
– 4 tablespoons thick heavy
  (double) cream
– 9 oz/250 g ready-to-bake
  puff pastry
– flour, for dusting
– 1 egg yolk, beaten with a
  little water
– salt and pepper

Preheat the oven to 350°F/180°C/Gas Mark 4. Heat the butter in a skillet or frying pan, add the garlic, and cook lightly, then discard it. Add all the blanched vegetables and cook briefly for a few minutes. season with salt and pepper, and stir in the cream.

Roll out the puff pastry into a thin rectangle on a lightly floured surface. Leaving a ½-inch/1-cm border round the edge, brush the surface with the remaining melted butter, and spread out the vegetables on top, then roll up the pastry like a strudel to form a roll. Pinch the ends of the pastry to seal them, brush the surface with the egg yolk, and bake for 30 minutes. Serve warm, cut into slices.

TORTA ARROTOLATA
DI CAROTE E ZUCCHINE
CARROT AND ZUCCHINI STRUDEL

AVERAGE

– Preparation time: *25 minutes*
– Cooking time: *1 hour*
– Calories per portion: *409*
– *Serves 6*

INGREDIENTS

– 4 tablespoons olive oil
– 1 shallot, finely chopped
– 4 cups (1 lb 5 oz/600 g)
  thinly sliced carrots
– 1 clove garlic, crushed
– 2 zucchini (courgettes),
  diced
– 9 oz/250 g ready-to-bake
  puff pastry
– all-purpose (plain) flour,
  for dusting
– 1½ oz/40 g fontina cheese,
  cut into strips
– ¾ cup (2 oz/60 g) grated
  Parmesan cheese
– 2 oz/60 g Gruyère cheese,
  thinly sliced
– 1 egg yolk, lightly beaten
  with a little water
– salt and pepper

Preheat the oven to 375°F/190°C/Gas Mark 5 and line a baking sheet with parchment (baking) paper. Heat 2 tablespoons oil in a saucepan, add the shallot, and cook until it is transparent, then add the carrots. Cook, stirring, for 5 minutes, then add a pinch of salt, cook for 5 minutes and remove from the heat.

Heat 2 tablespoons oil in another saucepan, add the garlic clove, and cook until lightly browned, then discard it. Add the zucchini (courgettes), stir, season with salt and pepper, and cook for another 10 minutes.

Meanwhile, roll out the puff pastry into a rectangle on a lightly floured surface and sprinkle the fontina cheese over it, leaving a ¾-inch/2-cm border around the edge. Sprinkle the carrots over the cheese, sprinkle with half the grated Parmesan, and cover this with a layer of zucchini. Place the Gruyère slices on top and sprinkle with the remaining grated Parmesan.

Roll up the pastry carefully into a strudel, brush the surface with the egg yolk, and place on the baking sheet. Bake for about 40 minutes, or until golden brown. Remove from the oven and serve warm on a serving plate, cut into slices.

ASPARAGI ARROTOLATI

ASPARAGUS ROLLS

EASY

– Preparation time: *40 minutes*
– Cooking time: *30 minutes*
– Calories per serving: *534*
– *Serves 4*

INGREDIENTS

– 11 oz/300 g ready-to-bake
  puff pastry
– all-purpose (plain) flour, for
  dusting
– 1 lb 2 oz/500 g asparagus
– 3 tablespoons (1½ oz/40 g)
  butter, melted
– 1 tablespoon grated
  Parmesan cheese
– 4 (2 oz/50 g) slices
  prosciutto (Parma ham)
– 4 (3½ oz/100 g) slices
  fontina cheese

Preheat the oven to 425°F/220°C/Gas Mark 7. Roll out the pastry on a lightly floured surface and cut it into four 6-inch/15-cm squares.

Steam the asparagus for 12 minutes, until tender, drain well, and arrange in a single layer on large plate. Sprinkle them with the butter and the grated Parmesan. Divide the asparagus into 4 bundles and wrap a slice of Parma ham, followed by a slice of fontina cheese, around each bundle. Place the bundles on the pastry squares and wrap the pastry around them, allowing the tips of the asparagus to protrude a little.

Place on a baking sheet lined with aluminum foil and bake for 15 minutes, until golden brown.

Tip: Before cooking the pastry bundles, you can cover the protruding asparagus tips with small pieces of foil to prevent them from drying out and becoming discolored while cooking.

TORTA ARROTOLATA DI CARCIOFI E ZUCCHINE

ARTICHOKE AND ZUCCHINI STRUDEL

AVERAGE

- Preparation time: *40 minutes*
- Cooking time: *1 hour 20 minutes*
- Calories per serving: *411*
- Serves 6

FOR THE STRUDEL

- 4 tablespoons olive oil
- 1 garlic clove, crushed
- 4 young, tender artichokes, trimmed and thinly sliced
- 2 zucchini (courgettes), trimmed and diced
- about ¼ cup (2 fl oz/50 ml) vegetable broth (stock)
- pinch of mace (optional)
- ¾ cup (7 oz/200 g) ricotta cheese
- 9 oz/250 g ready-to-bake puff pastry
- all-purpose (plain) flour, for dusting
- 1 egg, lightly beaten
- 1 tablespoon sesame seeds
- salt and pepper

FOR THE SAUCE

- 3 tablespoons (1¼ oz/30 g) butter
- ¼ cup (1¼ oz/30 g) flour
- 2 cups (18 fl oz/500 ml) hot vegetable broth (stock)
- ¼ oz/10 g dried porcini mushrooms, soaked
- ¼ cup (½ oz/15 g) finely chopped flat-leaf parsley
- salt and pepper

Preheat the oven to 375°F/190°C/Gas Mark 5 and line a large baking pan with parchment (baking) paper. Heat the oil in a Dutch oven or casserole dish, add the garlic, brown it lightly, then discard it. Add the artichokes and cook over high heat for 5 minutes. Add the zucchini (courgettes), broth (stock), and mace, if using, season with salt and pepper and cook for 10 minutes. Stir in the ricotta and remove from the heat.

Roll out the pastry into a large rectangle on a lightly floured surface, spread the ricotta and vegetable mixture out on it, and roll up the pastry into the shape of a strudel.

Mix the beaten egg with a little water. Brush the surface with the egg, mixture sprinkle with the sesame seeds, and cut diagonal incisions with a small, sharp knife. Transfer the strudel to the baking pan and bake for 40–45 minutes. Remove from the oven and let cool until just warm.

While it cools, make the sauce. Melt the butter in a saucepan, add the flour, and stir well. Keep stirring with a wire balloon whisk as you add the hot broth in a thin stream, then add the soaked, drained, squeezed and chopped mushrooms and cook, stirring, for 20 minutes. Season with salt and pepper and finally add the parsley. Serve slices of the strudel on individual plates, with 1–2 tablespoons of the hot sauce on the side.

TORTA PASQUALINA

TORTA PASQUALINA

– Preparation time: *1 hour*
– Cooking time: *1 hour*
– Calories per serving: *319*
– *Serves 8–10*

INGREDIENTS

– butter, for greasing
– olive oil, for brushing
– 1 oz/300 g cooked beets
  (beetroot), chopped
– 1⅓ cups (11 oz/300 g)
  ricotta cheese
– 2 tablespoons grated
  Parmesan cheese
– 2 tablespoons bread crumbs
– 8 eggs, 4 lightly beaten
– ¼ cup (2 fl oz/60 ml) light
  (single) cream
– sprig of fresh marjoram,
  chopped
– 14 oz/400 g ready-to-bake
  puff pastry
– flour, for dusting
– salt and pepper

Preheat the oven to 400°F/200°C/Gas Mark 6 and grease a baking sheet with butter. Push the ricotta cheese through a strainer (sieve) into a bowl and mix with the Parmesan, bread crumbs, the 4 beaten eggs, and the cream. Season with salt and pepper. Add the beets (beetroot) and, finally, the chopped marjoram.

Divide the pastry in half and roll out the first half into a 10-inch/25-cm disk, about ¼ inch/6 mm thick, on a lightly floured surface. Line the 7-inch/18-cm cake pan, creating a rim with the pastry around the edges, and brush with oil. Lay the second disk on top and pour over half the beet mixture. Make 4 wells in the vegetable mixture and crack an egg into each of them. Season with salt and pepper.

Pour over the other half of the beet mixture and smooth until even with a wet knife. Roll out the remaining pastry to 8-inch/20-cm disk, about ¼ inch/6 mm thick. Place on top of the filling and press down well around the edges and seal by folding over the pastry. Prick the top with a fork and bake for about 30 minutes. Cover the pastry with aluminum foil and bake for another 30 minutes.

Remove and rest it for about 10 minutes, then transfer to a serving dish and serve warm or cold.

Recipe Notes

Butter should always
be unsalted.

Eggs and fruits are assumed
to be large (UK: medium) size,
unless otherwise specified.

Milk is always whole
(full-fat), unless otherwise
specified.

Cooking and preparation
times are only for guidance,
as individual ovens vary. If
using a convection (fan) oven,
follow the manufacturer's
instructions concerning oven
temperatures.

Some recipes include
raw or very lightly cooked
eggs. These should be
avoided particularly by the
elderly, infants, pregnant
women, convalescents, and
anyone with an impaired
immune system.

All spoon measurements
are level. 1 teaspoon = 5 ml;
1 tablespoon = 15 ml. Australian standard tablespoons are
20 ml, so Australian readers
are advised to use 3 teaspoons
in place of 1 tablespoon
when measuring small
quantities.

Cup, imperial, and metric
measurements are given
throughout, and US equiva-
lents are given in brackets.
Follow one set of measurements, not a mixture, because
they are not interchangeable.

Phaidon Press Limited
Regent's Wharf
All Saints Street
London N1 9PA

Phaidon Press Inc.
65 Bleecker Street
New York, NY 10014

www.phaidon.com

First published 2015
© 2015 Phaidon Press Limited

ISBN: 978 07148 7001 4

Italian Cooking School Pizza originates from *Il cucchiaio d'argento estate*, first published in 2005; *Il cucchiaio d'argento cucina regionale*, first published in 2008; *Scuola di cucina Torte salate, pizze e focacce*, first published in 2013. © Editoriale Domus S.p.A. and Cucchiaio d'Argento S.r.l.

A CIP catalogue record for this book is available from the British Library.

Commissioning Editor: Emilia Terragni
Project Editor: Michelle Lo
Production Controller: Mandy Mackie
Designed by Atlas

Translation by First Edition Translations Ltd

Photography © Phaidon Press: Liz and Max Haarala Hamilton 6, 10, 23 ,24, 27, 31, 32, 35, 39, 47, 48, 52, 62, 69, 70, 73, 77, 81, 85, 90, 97, 98, 107, 112, 115, 117, 119, 123, 125, 128, 135, 40, 143, 147, 148, 151, 156, 159, 165, 166, 169, 173; Steven Joyce 130, 132; Edward Park 28, 36, 40; Andy Sewell 44, 121

Photography © Editoriale Domus S.p.A. and Cucchiaio d'Argento S.r.l.: Archivio Cucchiaio d'Argento s.r.l. 9, 13, 14, 18, 20, 43, 51, 56, 58, 61, 66, 74, 78, 82, 86, 89, 93, 94, 101, 104, 108, 111, 127, 136, 139, 144, 152, 155, 162, 170

Printed in Romania

The publisher would like to thank Carmen Figini, Ellie Smith, Astrid Stavro, Nuria Cabrera, Katie Blinman, Laura Gladwin, Theresa Beb-bington, Susan Spaull, and Vanessa Bird for their contributions to the book.